Married. Happily.

GREG LAURIE

Married. Happily.

Unless otherwise indicated, all Scripture quotations are taken from: *The Holy Bible, New King James Version* © 1984 by Thomas Nelson, Inc.

Scripture quotations marked (NIV) are from *The Holy Bible, New International Version*®, NIV®. Copyright © 1973, 1978, 1984 by International Bible Society. Used by permission of Zondervan Publishing House.

Scripture quotations marked (TLB) are taken from *The Living Bible*, Copyright © 1971 by Tyndale House Publishers, Wheaton, Illinois

Scripture quotations marked (NLT) are taken from *The New Living Translation*, Copyright © 1996, 2004 by Tyndale Charitable Trust. Used by permission of Tyndale House Publishers. All rights reserved.

Scripture quotations marked (MSG) are taken from *The Message*, by Eugene Peterson. 1993, 1994, 1995, 1996, 2000, 2001, 2002. Used by permission of NavPress Publishing Group. All rights reserved.

Scripture quotations marked (PHILLIPS) are from *The New Testament in Modern English, Revised Edition* © 1958, 1960, 1972 by J. B. Phillips.

Scripture quotations marked (AMPLIFIED) are taken from the *Amplified Bible*,® Copyright © 1954, 1958, 1962, 1964, 1965, 1987 by the Lockman Foundation. Used by permission. (www.Lockman.org)

International Standard Book Number: 978-0-9834004-2-4
Published by: Kerygma Publishing
Coordination: FM Management, Ltd.
www.kerygmapublishing.com
Contact: mgf@fmmgt.net
Cover Design: Mark Ferjulian and Greg Laurie
Production: Mark Ferjulian

Printed in India

3 4 5 6 7 8 9 / 20 19 18 17 16 15

To my best friend, closest confidant,
and wife of 38 years, Cathe.

Contents

CHAPTER 1

A Lifelong Lifestyle

Many waters cannot quench love; neither can rivers drown it. If a man tried to buy love with everything he owned, his offer would be utterly despised. –Song of Solomon 8:7, NLT

A pastor was invited to speak to a group of fourth-graders on the topic of marriage. As the children took their seats in the little wooden chairs, the preacher smiled and said, "Kids, I want to talk to you about marriage today. I wonder if any of you could tell me what God has to say about marriage."

Immediately one little boy waved his hand back and forth, so the pastor called on him. "Okay, son," he said, "what does God say about marriage?"

The boy replied, "Father, forgive them, for they know not what they do."

There are a lot of miserable people out there who have not found their marriages to be what they had expected. Maybe that's why one disillusioned soul wrote: "Marriage is like a three-ring circus: engagement ring, wedding ring, and suffering." If that describes your marriage right now, I want you to know that it can change.

By God's grace, I've had the privilege of being married to Cathe for 38 years now. Prior to getting married, we courted for three years. We wanted to really get to know each other. Apparently we were following the advice of Benjamin Franklin, who said, "Keep your eyes wide open before marriage, and half-shut afterwards."[1]

As I recall, we had a few dramatic disagreements and arguments during those three years. We also had big breakups. In fact, we broke up three times while we were courting. (It basically became an annual event.) But after spending time apart, we realized how much we truly loved each other, that we were miserable without each other, and that we were meant to be together.

Some people talk about "love at first sight" and seem to think it's a big deal. I've heard it said, "Love at first sight is nothing special. It's when two people have been looking at each other for years and still love each other that it becomes a miracle."

I've been looking at the same woman for 38 years, and frankly, she looks better to me all the time. Our love has only grown stronger through the years. The Bible says, "Many waters cannot quench love, nor can the floods drown it,"[2] and we have certainly found that to be the case in the Laurie home.

I remember the day we got married as though it were yesterday. I was 21; Cathe was 18. Walking down the aisle, she was a vision of beauty, dressed in radiant white. I distinctly remember a shaft of light coming through the window and shining through her veil. It looked like she was…glowing.

I, on the other hand, looked like a rerun of Grizzly Adams, with shoulder-length hair and a bushy red beard. Cathe tells me the same shaft of light I saw coming through her veil was also shining on my beard, which looked to her like a bright-red burning bush. To complete the package, I had somehow managed to rent the ugliest tuxedo ever made. I remember not wanting to get the "traditional" one, so I picked out one I had thought looked ultra-cool. Now as I look at those old photos, I ask myself, *What was I thinking?*

Thankfully, however, my wife could see that underneath all of that hair and the ridiculous tuxedo was a clean-shaven bald man who loved her—which she has today. We've both been so thankful to the Lord for His faithfulness to us through the years of our marriage.

My friend Franklin Graham says that each Christmas, when he receives our family photo, it's as though Cathe is frozen in time and I'm in an accelerated phase of aging. (Thanks, Franklin.) I'm just glad nobody has mistaken her for my daughter—yet.

Young as we were when we stood together at the altar, however, we had established our marriage on some important biblical principles—principles we've held to ever since.

While I'm certainly not an expert on marriage, I do know a little bit about marriage and divorce, because I have experienced both. I grew up in a broken home, with five different men in my life who were "fathers"—if you could call them that.

As a result, I know firsthand what it's like to experience the pain that divorce can bring into a person's life. Maybe that's one of the reasons that, to this very day, I have such a strong aversion to divorce—and want to do everything I can to steer married couples away from that direction if they are considering it.

A Strong Marriage Is No Accident

Tragically, we live in a time when intact families are becoming more and more of a rarity. And a flourishing marriage? Well, that's a downright oddity. But it doesn't have to be that way. God can bless your marriage, and make it every bit as happy and fulfilling as a Christian marriage of a hundred years ago.

In fact, that's the very thing He wants to do. After all, let's remember that God invented marriage, and nobody knows better than He about how it's supposed to function. And thrive.

For this reason, we must find those strong principles for healthy marriages that are given to us in Scripture, and follow them with all our hearts. I can say without hesitation that next to salvation itself, a marriage lived out according to God's design is the most wonderful and satisfying gift that you can find on this earth. That is why Proverbs 18:22 (NLT) says, "The man who finds a wife finds a treasure and receives favor from the LORD."

As the saying goes, "Marriage halves our grief, doubles our joys—and quadruples our expenses!" Maybe so, but it's worth every penny.

A strong and happy marriage is not only fulfilling spiritually, but emotionally benefiting as well. Research shows that people who are married live longer than those who are not. Records indicate that married men and women go to the doctor less often and make less use of other healthcare services than unmarried people. Virtually every study of mortality and marital status shows that the unmarried of both sexes have higher death rates, whether by accident, disease or self-inflicted wounds.

In fact, records dating back to the 19th century show that the highest suicide rates occur among the divorced, followed by widows and widowers, and those who never married. The lowest rates of suicide were among married people.[3]

Even with all of these potential benefits, however, marriage has not been a happy experience for everyone. Oil tycoon J. Paul Getty, one of the richest men who ever lived, said, "I would give my entire fortune for one happy marriage."[4] That's a tragic statement, isn't it? If you have a happy marriage today, then you have more than one of the world's wealthiest men ever had.

Yet having a strong, healthy marriage is no accident. It takes hard work. It's ironic to me that some folks spend more time planning for the wedding than for the actual marriage. Some people put more thought and effort into what they'll wear for a few hours on their wedding day than in thinking through how they will live and function for the rest of their married lives.

Could it be they don't really expect their marriage to last anyway?

Many of us remember the wedding of Charles, Prince of Wales, to Lady Diana Spencer on July 29, 1981. London was like a vast stage that day, with flowers everywhere. With great pomp and circumstance, Lady Di and her prince rode in royal carriages to the magnificent St. Paul's Cathedral. They recited their marriage vows to one another in the presence of the Queen, along with many VIPs and foreign dignitaries from around the world. The fairy-tale-like event was broadcast to a global audience of 750 million.

On that picture-perfect day, it would have been impossible to imagine the adversity that awaited this royal couple, from their highly publicized divorce to Diana's tragic death in 1997. Other than their two sons, basically all that remains of that union are the remnants of tabloid fodder.

Now Diana's son has had his own 'fairy-tale' wedding to Kate Middleton that was viewed by millions around the world.

It's been estimated that up to $40 Million was spent on this Fairy-Tale Wedding.

$32 Million on Security alone!

$600,000 was spent on a Luncheon and Dinner Reception.

Princess Kate's Wedding Gown and additional outfits she wore cost $434,000.

Let's hope that marriage fares better then William's parents, Charles and Diana.

The Age of Drive-Thru Divorce

We all know the phrase "a marriage made in heaven"—which almost implies that some marriages seem to work out just fine, while others are doomed from the start. It's as if to say, "Hopefully your marriage will be one of those made in heaven. But if it doesn't, no problem. Just bail out. It doesn't matter. You'll do better next time." Meanwhile, the divorce rate continues to spiral out of control.

It is this very cavalier attitude about marriage that not only destroys families, but eats away at the very fabric of our country. Today, the United States leads the world with the most divorces in a monogamous nation.[5] You can get drive through weddings and now drive through divorces as well.

So, how does that work out I wonder.

You order your lunch at the drive through window and ask "Could I get some fries as well as a *divorce* with that?"

Meanwhile, this breakdown of the family is having a devastating impact on our nation. According to the National Fatherhood Initiative, children of divorce are more likely to "be suspended from school, or to drop out; be treated for an emotional or behavioral problem; commit suicide as adolescents; and be victims of child abuse or neglect" than children of intact families.[6]

The problem is that we treat marriage as something disposable. What particularly concerns me is that this same mentality has found its way into the church. I have seen far too many marriages dissolved for no good reason.

I will grant that, in a very small number of situations, people have divorced who should have done so. But in my experience as a pastor for almost four decades, I have found that most marriages that ended in divorce had no biblical grounds for it, and *did not need to fall apart*. Rather, they fell apart due to neglect and a lack of obedience to the clear biblical teaching on marriage. When we tamper with God's plan, we do so at our own peril.

If you want a good marriage, you can have one. But as I said, it takes work—and lots of it. If you want a bad marriage, you can have that as well—simply through neglect and allowing it to drift along and "find its own way." God has given us effective, enduring principles in His Word, and we will explore and work through these together in this book. Right from the start, however, we will need strength beyond our own.

If you truly want this book to be a real force in your life for bringing help, healing, and renewal to your marriage, I suggest you do this: Set the book down for a few moments, and ask God's Holy Spirit to speak to you, teach you, strengthen you, and enable you with power, patience and perseverance beyond your own.

Build on the Right Foundation

Marriage is a lot like a mirror—it gives back a reflection of you. At my age, I'm not crazy about mirrors, and I spend as little time as possible looking into one. Frankly, they show me some things I'd rather not see.

When it comes to your marriage, you make it into what it is. If you don't like what you're seeing in the marital mirror, then it's time to do something about it.

We have to return to God's plan and God's principles. These principles haven't been given to some imaginary spiritual elite, but to ordinary people like you and me—people who live in this real world and face real challenges.

Living in the time and the culture that we do, our marriages must deal with obstacles and challenges that our parents, grandparents and great-grandparents never had to face. They had some pretty serious issues of their own, though, including world wars, a devastating worldwide economic depression, and the growing shadow of nuclear annihilation.

The fact is, the Bible speaks to every generation. Its principles are every bit as true and as relevant as they were one hundred— even one thousand—years ago.

The book of Hebrews gives us this graphic image:

For the word of God is full of living power. It is sharper than the sharpest knife, cutting deep into our innermost thoughts and desires. It exposes us for what we really are. Nothing in all creation can hide from him. Everything is naked and exposed before his eyes. This is the God to whom we must explain all that we have done. (Hebrews 4:12-13, NLT)

In addition to everything else, the Bible is a practical book. Not only is it the inspired Word of God, but it's also a book that speaks to real life. It tells us how to live.

Jesus said, "Therefore whoever hears these sayings of Mine, and does them, I will liken him to a wise man who built his house on the rock: and the rain descended, the floods came, and the winds blew and beat on that house; and it did not fall, for it was founded on the rock" (Matthew 7:24–25).

Storms will come into every life, every marriage, every family. As the saying goes, into every life a little rain must fall. In some lives, a lot of rain falls—and sometimes it feels more like a hurricane. If your marriage is built on a solid foundation, you will come through the storms stronger as a result. But if your marriage is built on a weak foundation of sand, symbolizing those who hear the Word but don't obey it, the storms will devastate you.

It's a whole lot easier to lay the foundation right the first time, and then build on it, than it is to redo a faulty foundation while you're living in the house.

I've never built a house, but I have remodeled. People who have built their houses have told me it is far easier to build than to remodel. Maybe you will have to do a little remodeling of your marriage. It will be hard, yes. But it is *infinitely* better than the alternative, which is having your marriage become one more sad statistic in the failure column.

A good way for Christians to begin in their effort to have a healthy and strong marriage is to strike the word "divorce" from their vocabularies. Don't consider it, don't contemplate it, don't entertain the idea of it, and don't ever bring it up.

Yes, I'm aware the Bible gives certain grounds for divorce, which I'll discuss later on. I realize there are situations where it is justified and understandable. But once again, I want to emphasize that the vast majority of divorces today don't have to happen. Our culture tends to view divorce as a convenient escape hatch when things get tough, and we resort to it far too readily.

We ought to say, "Divorce isn't even on the table. We won't consider it as an option, period. We will honor our vows, which were for better or for worse, for richer or poorer, in sickness and health, to love and to cherish, until death do us part."

If you have made such vows, you *can* keep them with the help and power of Almighty God. It's time to turn the tide in our nation.

Victory Isn't Won by Evacuation

You may be thinking, *You're dreaming, Greg. It's too late for marriage in our culture. You can't turn back time.* Maybe not. But I'm reminded of the question, "How do you eat an elephant?" And the answer, of course, is *one bite at a time*.

So how do we turn around this devastating trend in our country?

One marriage at a time. One family at a time.

If every couple would say, "By the grace of God, this will *not* happen in our home. We're drawing a line right here, and we will make our stand."

During World War II, when England was bombarded nightly by the Nazis, the people of that island nation began to despair of life. Some actually wanted the prime minister, Winston Churchill, to surrender. That great British leader, of course, flatly rejected such a cowardly course of action. "Wars," he insisted, "are not won by evacuations."[7]

We can apply that same truth to marriage. Victory will never be won by evacuation. Running away, giving up, or waving the white flag may seem like the easiest path out of stress and heartache, but it will only bring greater devastation.

We must determine to persevere.

And we never have to do it alone.

Questions for Discussion

1. Greg quotes Song of Solomon 8:7 (NLT): *"Many waters cannot quench love; neither can rivers drown it."*

What are the "many waters" and "rivers" in today's world that would seek to drown and extinguish married love?

[handwritten notes]

2. Talk about the wisdom of Benjamin Franklin's quote on marriage: *"Keep your eyes wide open before marriage, and half-shut afterwards."*

[handwritten notes]

3. Greg writes that even though he and Cathe were very young when they married, they had determined to establish their home on strong biblical principles before they walked down the aisle. What is the advantage of starting out with some firm principles already in place? *[handwritten notes]*

4. Proverbs 18:22 (NLT) reads, *"The man who finds a wife finds a treasure and receives favor from the LORD."* Thinking of your own spouse, take a moment to describe what that "treasure" and "favor" looks like in your life. How has our culture made this treasure to look less and less valuable and important? How can we counteract our culture's trend of degrading and belittling marriage and family?

[handwritten notes]

5. Greg writes: *"Some people will put more effort into what they will be wearing for a few hours on their wedding day than in thinking through how they will live and function for the rest of their married lives."*

If you aren't yet married, how does this statement make you stop and think about your plans? If you're already married, what sort of plans can you make to improve and strengthen your relationship?

effort instead of ring
assume positive not negative

6. *"If you want a bad marriage,"* Greg says, *"you can have that as well—simply through neglect and allowing it to drift along and find its own way."*

What are the problems/dangers associated with a passive approach to marriage—simply allowing it to "find its own way"?

no plan never works
must have goal a plan

7. Greg writes: *"Marriage is a lot like a mirror—it gives back a reflection of you."*

What do you see in that "reflection" that concerns you? What do you see that encourages you?

Easier do not talk then fight

the bought the books

8. It's difficult to "remodel" a marriage, just as it's difficult to remodel a house. What are some parallels that come to mind? When someone is planning to remodel a house or a room, what are the first steps? Again, are there parallels in remodeling a marriage? What are the potential pitfalls or discouraging circumstances in any remodeling task?

Plan

9. Greg writes that Christian couples need to *"strike the word divorce from their vocabularies."* How would such a mindset strengthen the marriage relationship?

CHAPTER 2
Marriage Is God's Idea

And the LORD God said, "It is not good that man should be alone; I will make him a helper comparable to him." –Genesis 2:18

Sometimes we imagine the Garden of Eden almost like a fairy tale, like Camelot, Atlantis or Never-Never Land. But the Bible gives us a historical account of events that actually happened. These were real events in a real place in a real time.

We need to remember that Genesis, the first of the five books of Moses known as the Pentateuch, was written to the people of Israel during the days of their wilderness wandering in the Sinai Desert. God was the eyewitness, and He gave these words to His servant Moses, the author of Genesis.

Eden was no myth or fairyland. The Bible identifies it as an actual piece of real estate, and we're even given some GPS coordinates—well, something like that. Genesis 2:8 tells us, "The LORD God planted a garden eastward," locating it near the area of the present-day Tigris and Euphrates Rivers. If you had lived in that era, and could have had a computer with you, you could have located it on Google Earth.

We also read in Genesis 2:11 of places called Pishon and the land of Havilah. While we don't know for certain where these places were, the fact that they are mentioned shows that these were actual geographical places.

A Place of Perfection

The whole world must have been beautiful and lush before

Adam and Eve's fall, but the Garden was something really special. Think of all of the gorgeous places you've ever seen—every vision of every tropical isle on every travel brochure. Eden surpassed all of those. Eden was perfection.

In the midst of this earthly paradise was the Tree of Life. We later learn that the fruit of this tree, if eaten, allowed you to live forever. That is why, after Adam and Eve ate of the Tree of the Knowledge of Good and Evil, God made sure they could not eat of the Tree of Life. The Creator would not allow Adam and Eve to live forever in their fallen state.

Interestingly enough, we're told that in the New Jerusalem we will eventually have access to this tree. Revelation 22:2 says, "In the middle of its street, and on either side of the river, was the tree of life, which bore twelve fruits, each tree yielding its fruit every month. The leaves of the tree were for the healing of the nations."

So there was Adam, living in Eden, with everything that was pleasing to the eye and good for food (see Genesis 2:9). Adam's job was to "tend and keep" that beautiful garden (v. 15). This doesn't mean he was a glorified gardener, walking around clipping grass and trimming hedges. The Hebrew word used here for "keep" is a word that means "discover its secrets."

And who can even imagine how many wonderful secrets God had built into this wondrous garden?

God said, "Adam, I have put this here for you to enjoy. I want you to walk around and behold My glory. I want you to see My handiwork and just have a great time. I will be there every day to walk with you and have fellowship with you.

"But there's just one thing, Adam. There is a special tree that I've created over at the center of the Garden. I don't want you to eat any of the fruit from that tree." It was clear God had established parameters. So Adam just walked around, taking in all the beauty of what God had created.

The Lord created animal life, and it was Adam's job to name them. Think of all the strange creatures in the world—Adam had to come up with a name for each of them. I wonder if he started running out of ideas after a while.

"Let's see. . .I'll call that one dog, that one cat, that one bird, and that one fish. . ."What, I have to have individual names for each fish?

Okay, Salmon, Trout, Swordfish, Halibut, Mahi. . . .uh. . Mahi- Mahi!"

Maybe Adam just gave up when he came up with the fish name "Humuhumunuk Unukuapuaa"(Apparently the longest fish name).

But as wondrous and beautiful as everything was, there was still something missing in Adam's life. If you'd asked him at the time, I don't think he could have said what that vague sense of incompleteness was all about. The truth was, Adam longed for a someone who hadn't even been created yet.

God, however, knew every secret of Adam's heart. He said, "It is not good that man should be alone; I will make him a helper comparable to him" (v. 18).

A Match Made in Heaven

Again and again in Genesis 1 we encounter the phrase, "And God saw that it was good."

But God saw Adam's loneliness, and He said that it is "not good." This was the first time that God looked at His creation and said that something wasn't good. "*It is not good that man should be alone*" (2:18).

Why did God bring woman to man? This is a very important question to answer. Why does He bring us together as men and women? The answer is in Genesis 2:18: "I will make him a helper comparable to him." The Hebrew word for "helper" can be translated to mean "someone who assists another to reach fulfillment." It was used elsewhere in the Old Testament in reference to someone coming to the rescue of another. So Eve, in a very real sense, came to rescue Adam from his loneliness. God says that she is "comparable" to Adam, or corresponding to him.

This is important, because we live in a time and a culture that seeks to blur the differences between men and women. The assertion is that if certain social conditioning factors were changed, we would find that men and women are really the same. But that simply isn't true.

After huge and involved social experimentation in the 1960s and '70s, researchers finally concluded that boys are boys and girls are girls. (I could have told them that and saved all that time and money.) If we fail to recognize—and appreciate—this basic reality, we're really being very foolish.

It doesn't mean that one gender is better than the other. Men are not better than women, and women are not better than men. No, they are *different*. And both have been uniquely created in God's image.

In his book *Love for a Lifetime*, Dr. James Dobson cites some of the physiological differences between men and women. He points out that men and women differ in every cell of their body. For instance, a woman has greater constitutional vitality because of the chromosome difference. She usually outlives a man by three or four years, and in some cases, much longer. They also differ in their metabolism. Women have slower metabolisms than men, and different skeletal structures. Women have a shorter head, a broader face, a less protrusive chin, shorter legs and a longer trunk. Women have a larger stomach, liver, kidneys and appendix, and have smaller lungs. In brute strength, men are 50 percent stronger than women.[8]

We are different and God *made* us that way. It's all a part of our Creator's good and wise plan.

Somehow Adam and Eve managed to meet each other in the Garden without the benefit of an online dating service. Genesis 2 records the actual moment of that first encounter.

And the LORD God caused a deep sleep to fall on Adam, and he slept; and He took one of his ribs, and closed up the flesh in its place. Then the rib which the LORD God had taken from man He made into a woman, and He brought her to the man. And Adam said: "This is now bone of my bones and flesh of my flesh; she shall

be called Woman, because she was taken out of Man.
(Genesis 2:21–23)

Adam fell into a sleep, and when he awoke, there was Eve. He said, "This is now bone of my bones and flesh of my flesh." That might sound a little flat or prosaic in English, but in the original Hebrew, you can almost hear that garden rock with joy. His response was more like, "Yes! This is *good*! Lord, I love it!"

Eve was perfect in every way for Adam. At last, Adam had a partner. Someone with whom he could share his life, his thoughts and his joys. (He didn't have any concerns or worries to share at that point.)

Marriage: God's Design

So God brought Adam and Eve together and established marriage with the immortal words: "Therefore shall a man leave his father and his mother, and shall cleave unto his wife: and they shall be one flesh" (v. 24, KJV).

It's interesting to note that Jesus quotes this statement in the New Testament. The Pharisees came to Him and asked, "Is it lawful for a man to divorce his wife for just any reason?" (Matthew 19:3). Quoting from Genesis, Jesus replied, "Have you not read that He who made them at the beginning 'made them male and female' … 'For this reason a man shall leave his father and mother and be joined to his wife, and the two shall become one flesh'?" (Matthew 19:4-5).

Long before there was a nation, a government, a school or even a church, there was a man and woman brought together to be husband and wife. The institution of marriage predates every other human institution or relationship in Scripture, and remains one of the key foundation stones of any society.

Genesis 2:24 provides some essential truths regarding God's design for marriage. In fact, two words sum it up: *leaving* and *cleaving*. First you must leave. Then you must cleave.

It begins with leaving.

Marriage begins with a leaving—a distinct departure and

distancing from all other relationships. The closest relationship outside of marriage is specified here, which is the relationship of a child to his parents. This implies that if it's necessary to leave your father and mother, then all lesser ties must be broken, changed or left behind. You leave all other relationships.

Yes, you are still a son or a daughter to your parents, but it is different now, because you have been joined to your spouse. Your relationship with your parents has changed. A new family has been established. Once he is married, the man's primary commitment is to his wife, and her primary commitment is to him.

Sadly, what happens in many marriages is that this vital process of leaving never takes place. One or both parties think, *If things don't work out, I'll go home to Mommy.* Or maybe, *If things don't work out, I'll go back to my old friends and hang out with them.* People who think this way have never really left other relationships, and haven't chosen to cleave to their spouse.

You need to learn to work things out as husband and wife. You need to learn how to communicate. And yes, you need to learn how to *disagree*.

During my initial premarital counseling session with a couple, I will ask, "Have you two had a fight yet?" (Not a fist fight, but a disagreement.)

"No," some reply. "We *never* argue."

And then I'll surprise them and say, "Okay, you need to get out of here then, because I'm not going to marry you. Go have a few arguments, and then we can talk."

The fact is, you have to learn how to agreeably disagree. You have to learn what to do in situations where you don't see eye to eye. You need to know how to wrestle with an issue as a couple, how to resolve your differences, and how to forgive one another. Without learning these vital lessons, you are in danger of turning every disagreement into a battle, and you'll begin to resent each other.

If you are a husband, your best friend and closest confidant needs to be your wife. If you are a wife, the same needs to be true of your husband. It's good to have other friends, but there should only be one best friend in your life, and it should be your spouse.

It becomes especially dangerous when a wife has male friends other than her husband, and a husband has female friends other than his wife. Whether we will it or not, we begin bonding with these people. Before you know it, this "innocent friendship" isn't quite so innocent anymore, and can lead into the devastation of adultery.

Most adulterous relationships, especially in the case of women, did not begin with sexual attraction. They began because a woman felt her husband wasn't giving her the attention she wanted and wasn't spending time with her. So she developed a friendship with a man who would show some interest.

"We're just friends," she might explain. "It's nothing more. He understands me. I understand him. We encourage one another. We pray together. We read the Bible together."

But understand this: *It's not going to work*.

"We're just friends" will change into something else—and that change can happen more quickly than you might imagine.

The same goes for men. A man might say, "This lady at work—we really understand each other. We talk about everything. She's not my wife; she's just a buddy."

Watch out! Never underestimate the power of emotional and physical attraction between a man and a woman. Before you know it, you'll find yourself entangled in a relationship you never meant to get involved in.

Husbands, make your wife your best friend. Wives, make your husband your best friend. Cultivate the friendship in your marriage. After all, the very purpose of marriage from the beginning was companionship.

Yes, sexual intimacy is a big and wonderful part of the equation—a way to express the oneness that exists between a man and a woman. But that aspect, too, ought to be built on friendship and warm companionship.

Those who have been in good marriages for many years will tell you that. Those who have been widowed and later remarried will say, "It's so good to do things together—going to the grocery store, washing the car, just sitting together on the couch and watching an old movie, whatever. It's so good not to be alone anymore."

It's sad to see friendship lost in a marriage.

The husband and wife may be lovers, good parents to their children, and an efficient, working team getting through life's demands. But it is so very sad if they have forgotten what it means to be *friends*. They have forgotten what it's like to bare their hearts. They have forgotten to keep one another updated on what's going on in their lives.

Sometimes you see a couple in a restaurant, eating in the same booth but never looking at or saying a word to each other. It's so obvious the friendship has gone out of their relationship (if it was ever really there) and they simply have nothing to say to one another.

How very sad. And lonely!

Soon, that lack of friendship begins to affect everything else in the marriage, and they begin to drift apart.

Listen to what God says in Malachi 2:14: "The LORD has been witness between you and the wife of your youth, with whom you have dealt treacherously; yet she is your companion and your wife by covenant." Note the words "companion" and "wife." That word "companion" can be translated from the Hebrew to mean "one you are united with in thoughts, goals, plans and efforts." God is saying that we should be unified with our spouse in thoughts, goals, plans and efforts.

Then in 1 Peter 3, we read, "Husbands, likewise, dwell with them with understanding, giving honor to the wife, as to the weaker vessel, and as being heirs together of the grace of life, that your prayers may not be hindered" (v. 7). The word Peter used for "dwell" means "to be aligned to or to give maintenance to."

So to put it all together, we hear God saying, "Be aligned, and give maintenance to your wife. Be united with her in thoughts, goals, plans and efforts."

We think nothing of maintaining our cars or our garden, but it comes as a shock to us that our marriage needs maintenance as well!

What happens if you never maintain a car?

It will break down.

What happens if you neglect your garden?

It will be overrun with weeds.

And what happens if you do not maintain your marriage?

It, too, will break down.

For this reason, I must periodically take stock of my life and ask myself if there is any relationship or pursuit I'm involved in that would put distance between me and my mate. Is anything getting in the way of our closeness? Anything at all? My career, perhaps? My hobby? My obsession with this or that? Is there anything in my life that might be crowding or damaging my relationship with my spouse?

If there is, *take action!*

Friendship, companionship and closeness form the foundation of marriage. Every other relationship in your life must work in proportion with the relationship between you and your spouse. Yes, there's a place for buddies. There's a place for hobbies. There's a place for involvement in church activities. There's a place for business. But you shouldn't let anything obstruct your relationship with your spouse. That is all a part of "leaving."

But then Scripture says there must be a *cleaving*. It's no use leaving unless you are willing to spend a lifetime cleaving.

Leaving followed by cleaving

The very purpose of marriage in the beginning was companionship. The word used in Genesis 2:24 for "cleave" means "to adhere to, to stick to, to be attached by some strong tie." You may be thinking, That's me, all right. I'm stuck.

But that's not what this word means. In the verb form, it speaks of something that is done aggressively—a determined action. It's actually the idea of holding onto something. That is, it's not that you're just stuck to something, like a fly in a web, trying to get free. This is something you deliberately grip and hold, hanging on for dear life.

The word "cleave" speaks of a determined action. If you were walking along a cliff, suddenly lost your footing, fell over the edge, and grabbed a branch as you fell, you would cleave to that branch, because it's something you very much want to do! Why? Because your very life would depend on it.

That's the idea of the word "cleave" as used here. You and your spouse aren't holding onto each other passively, but aggressively. You are not 'stuck' together as much as you are sticking together. This is what needs to happen in our marriages. It's a sometimes slippery, stormy world out there, and we need to hang on to each other.

Let's face it—there are so many pressures that seek to pull a husband and wife apart these days. Staying together, then, needs to be a determined action. Imagine you're walking with your spouse up a steep hillside covered with slippery wet grass on a windy day. You'd hold onto each other, wouldn't you? In the same way, husbands and wives need to take deliberate action to cling to one another and to stay away from anything that might come between them.

That's the idea here in the Hebrew.

When you come to the New Testament use of the same word in the Greek language, it means "to cement together, to stick like glue, or to be welded together so the two cannot be separated without serious damage to both."

Therefore, we must periodically take stock in our lives and ask ourselves, *Is there any relationship or pursuit I'm currently involved in that would put distance between my mate and me? Is this thing that I am doing drawing us together or driving us apart? Will it build up our relationship or tear it down?*

It's not always the big things that bring a marriage down. Certainly there are big problems, such as unfaithfulness or abuse, that can destroy a marriage quickly. But it's the little things, over time, that often bring the marriage down.

As Song of Solomon says, it's "the little foxes that spoil the vines" (2:15). In a marriage, it can be a matter of neglecting the principle of leaving and cleaving. When there is an unwillingness to hold on tightly to your spouse, your marriage can begin to weaken. Problems can develop. So cleave to your spouse, recognizing that all other relationships must be secondary.

An integral part of this companionship is communication. I'm not sure I really believe it, but I've read that the average woman speaks 50,000 words a day, while the average man, 25,000 a day.[9] He probably uses up about 24,840 of those words at work. That means he's got about 160 words left when he gets home. Words like *food...TV remote...sleepy.*

One thing I like to do is communicate with my wife throughout the day. I call her up, or drop her an email or a text. I like to tell her what's going on, and bring her up to speed, and she does the same for me.

Here's what amazes me. Sometimes I'll relate a conversation or experience that happened to me at the office or on one of my trips. Then, maybe weeks later, I'll hear her describing my experience to someone else. She describes it so vividly and accurately that I ask myself, *Was she with me there? No, she couldn't have been. How does she know all this?*

The fact is, she just knows me. She knows what I mean when I say certain words. She reads things into the tone of my voice. We've been husband and wife for 38 years, and we know each other.

All too often, however, a marriage will face a breakdown in communication. Unless those breaks are soon mended, it can begin to damage the relationship.

I heard about an elderly husband and wife who had been married for many years. They were sitting together at the breakfast table. In a sudden, impulsive burst of loving emotion, he said, "Honey, I'm so proud of you."

His wife, however, was hard of hearing, and had misplaced

her hearing aid.

"What's that?" she said.

"Honey, I'm so proud of you."

"What's that?"

"Honey, I'm so PROUD of you."

"I can't hear you."

"Honey, I'M PROUD OF YOU."

"Well," she huffed, "I'm tired of you, too."

Yes, there are communication problems along the way, as there will be between any two human beings. But a man and a woman who have determined in their hearts to cleave together—no matter what—will find a way to rebuild every damaged bridge and reopen every blocked path.

God will help, if we ask Him.

He wants us to leave and cleave even more than we do.

Questions for Discussion

1. God said, *"It is not good that man should be alone; I will make him a helper comparable to him"* (Genesis 2:18). What does this verse imply about the companionship God intended from the very beginning for a husband and wife?

partner in all things — support each other
respect & happiness

2. Greg writes that the words "a helper comparable to him" could be translated from the Hebrew as *"someone who assists another to reach fulfillment."* List some of the ways we do that for one another in our marriages.

support goals   pick battles
compromise
respect & happiness

3. The chapter states that the *"institution of marriage predates every other human institution or relationship in Scripture."* How has the importance—the primacy—of this institution been diminished or degraded by today's culture? How can we as believers reestablish the once high position and value of marriage with the upcoming generations?

TV shows   walk the walk
celebrity lifestyles
divorce the easy

4. Read again Genesis 2:24. Describe the importance of "leaving" before "cleaving" in a marriage. What happens in a marriage when that leaving is only partial?

put priority in marriage
resentment & hurt feelings

5. Why does Greg say he won't marry a couple until they've had their first big fight?

couples need to agree to disagree
without hurt or thinking
thats a real healthy marriage

6. Why is it so important that your spouse should also be your best friend? What are some ways to really *cultivate* that friendship?

Best friends can relate hard without judging
Time discussion prayer

7. What are the dangers associated with husbands and wives not paying enough attention to one another?

straying. finding someone who will

8. People who have been widowed talk about missing doing the little things together—going to the grocery store, taking walks, preparing a meal, even doing the laundry. How can we gain a fresh perspective on the importance of just being with each other and "doing life" together?

tough one for me

9. Malachi 2:14 says: *"The LORD has been witness between you and the wife of your youth, with whom you have dealt treacherously; yet she is your companion and your wife by covenant."*

Greg writes that the Hebrew word translated as "companion" means "one you are united with in thoughts, goals, plans, and efforts." To what extent do those words describe your relationship with your spouse? If you're not experiencing that sort of companionship in your marriage, what are some practical ways you make progress in that direction?

Not much

discuss individual goals to find common ground

10. What are some of the areas of life that could potentially distract you from making companionship a high priority in your marriage?

together ~~the~~ other just &my times things

11. Greg says that the word "cleave" in marriage speaks of a determined action. It means you deliberately grip or hold on to your mate, not allowing possessions, preoccupations or other people to come between you. Why does this seem to be such a challenge to so many in today's world? How can you and your spouse regain this closeness if you sense you might be losing it?

independant. busy, Kids

Set aside time

CHAPTER 3
Why It's Hard Work

Lead a life worthy of your calling, for you have been called by God. Be humble and gentle. Be patient with each other, making allowance for each other's faults because of your love. Always keep yourselves united in the Holy Spirit, and bind yourselves together with peace.
–Ephesians 4:1-3, NLT

God wants to bless our marriages. After all, it was God who designed marriage. He originated it, He has uniquely established it, and He has given it as a blessing to humanity.

Because of this, one of Satan's greatest goals in our culture and in this time in which we live is to destroy as many marriages as he possibly can. And he doesn't much care whether those couples are Christians or not.

If he or his demons can find a crack or a crevice in a marriage and somehow gain a foothold, they'll try to exploit it to the max. As Paul told the church in Ephesus, "If you are angry, don't sin by nursing your grudge. Don't let the sun go down with you still angry—get over it quickly; *for when you are angry, you give a mighty foothold to the devil*" (Ephesians 4:26-27, TLB).

The evil one is looking for handholds, footholds, toeholds, any kind of holds in your marriage. He has set his sights on the family, and nothing would delight him more than to see it destroyed—especially Christian families. That is why we want to do everything we can to draw a line around our homes and say, "This belongs to the Lord. We will do this God's way, building our marriage on God's principles."

Looking Out for Number One

There's no use denying it: We live in a culture that is openly hostile to the institutions of marriage and the family. Activists do everything in their power to undermine and redefine what marriage and family really are. Using the tools of humor and cynicism, novelists, songwriters and TV- and movie-writers deliberately mock and ridicule traditional roles, values and families.

What's the alternative? *It is to seek your own happiness and pleasure, no matter what the cost.* We are essentially told to believe, "Everything revolves around me. I am the only one who ultimately matters."

Concepts like sacrifice, selflessness and keeping one's commitment are rarely heard of today, and we carry this same, selfish, "me-first" mentality into our marriages. We say, "I will marry you so you can make me a happy person. As long as you fulfill me and meet my needs, I will stay with you—that is, unless someone better or more interesting comes along."

We might not come right out and say that, but judging by the way many people act and behave today, it is reality.

Understand what I'm saying here. I'm not suggesting you can't be happy and fulfilled in a marriage. I'm saying that if you enter into marriage with the sole expectation of your spouse meeting *your* needs, and without any real concern about your meeting *theirs*, you will be disappointed.

Marriage depends on two things: finding the right person and being the right person.

The right motive is wanting to marry someone so you can make them happy, meet their needs and bring them fulfillment. That should be the motive. Yet self-obsession is so prevalent in our society today. In fact, the Bible tells us it would be paramount in the last days, a time in which I believe we are now living.

According to 2 Timothy 3,

In the last days perilous times will come: For men will be lovers of themselves, lovers of money, boasters, proud, blasphemers, disobedient to parents, unthankful, unholy, unloving, unforgiving, slanderers, without self-control, brutal, despisers of good, traitors,

headstrong, haughty, lovers of pleasure rather than lovers of God.
(*vv. 1–4*, emphasis mine)

Maybe you're thinking, *Wait a second. I thought we needed to love ourselves. I've always heard that the biggest problem in our culture was a lack of self-love. I thought that all of the problems of our culture could be traced to low self-esteem and poor self-image.*

Or so we are led to believe.

But the Bible tells us that one of the signs of the last days is that people will love themselves more than they love God. And it is because of our self-love—our fixation and obsession with self—that we find ourselves facing so many problems and heartaches in today's culture. In our entertainment-saturated society, we are living in an altered state of reality. We live with illusions of what life should be—the fantasy of the perfect romantic and sexual relationship…the perfect spouse…the perfect lifestyle.

Yet what we're chasing after doesn't even exist.

And when life doesn't measure up to what we think it should, we simply say, "I'll go and look for it somewhere else." This often includes bailing out on a marriage.

A Higher Calling

As Christians, we must abandon this unbiblical and destructive type of thinking. God has called us, as His children, to a different standard. He has called us to a higher level of living, a new way of thinking and behaving.

Ephesians 4:1–2 tells us, "Walk worthy of the calling with which you were called, with all lowliness and gentleness, with longsuffering, bearing with one another in love." As Christians, we cannot think as this world thinks or act as it acts. God says, "Come out from among them and be separate" (2 Corinthians 6:17).

Romans 12:2 (PHILLIPS) reads, "Don't let the world around you squeeze you into its own mould, but let God re-mould your minds from within, so that you may prove in practice that the plan of God for you is good, meets all his demands and moves towards the goal of true maturity."

With God's help, we must reject selfishness, and in its place find a new, selfless, God-honoring life in which we put God's Word above our own desires. If we want our marriages to be strong, we must value obedience to God and the needs of our spouse on a distinctly higher scale than our own wants and wishes.

While our culture tells us that self-esteem ought to be our brightest and most important guiding star, the Bible tells us otherwise:

> *Let nothing be done through selfish ambition or conceit, but in lowliness of mind let each* esteem others *better than himself. Let each of you look out not only for his own interests, but also for the interests of others. (Philippians 2:3–4, emphasis mine).*

If every married couple did this alone, our homes would be transformed overnight. If you put the needs of your wife or husband above your own, and thought of their happiness and their fulfillment over yours, it would radically change your home.

And all that happiness that you give will flow right back on you.

What Started It All

This, of course, not only flies in the face of cultural norms and expectations, but it also moves crosscurrent to our basic human nature. It all goes back to a very, very dark day in that paradise called Eden.

> *Now the serpent was more cunning than any beast of the field which the LORD God had made. And he said to the woman, "Has God indeed said, 'You shall not eat of every tree of the garden'?" And the woman said to the serpent, "We may eat the fruit of the trees of the garden; but of the fruit of the tree which is in the midst of the garden, God has said, 'You shall not eat it, nor shall you touch it, lest you die.'" Then the serpent said to the woman, "You will not surely die. For God knows that in the day you eat of it your eyes will be opened, and you will be like God, knowing good and evil." So when the woman saw that the tree was good for food, that it was pleasant to the eyes, and a tree desirable to make one wise, she took of its fruit and ate. She also gave to her husband with her, and he ate. Then the eyes of both of them were opened. (Genesis 3:1–7)*

Eve was at the wrong place at the wrong time, listening to the wrong voice, which led her to do the wrong thing. Adam soon joined her, and when confronted by God for an explanation of his disobedience, he gave the first excuse recorded in human history.

Adam said, "The woman whom You gave to be with me, she gave me of the tree, and I ate" (v. 12).

What a lame, cowardly thing to say.

You and I weren't there to hear the inflections of his voice, so we don't know how he spoke these words. (With a whine, maybe?) It could have come down to which word he emphasized in that sentence. For instance, if Adam said, "It's the woman You gave me," he was placing the blame on Eve, not himself. Conversely, if he said, "It's the woman You gave me," he would have been blaming God Himself. Either way, it was a pitiful excuse. Adam was fully responsible for his own actions.

Eve didn't fare much better as she tried to blame it all on Satan, as if she'd had nothing to do with it. "The serpent deceived me, and I ate" (v. 13). Loose paraphrase: "It's not my fault; the devil made me do it."

But there was no excuse. Adam and Eve both crossed the line, knowing only too well that it was the wrong thing to do. As a result of that sin, a curse came upon humanity, and we feel its repercussions to this very day. As a result of this curse, a number of very dark things entered into the human race, starting with death, the darkest of all.

A Terrible New Reality

Up to this point, Adam and Eve would not have faced death, disease or the aging process. But because of their sin, the curse of sickness, a limited lifespan, and the ultimate termination of life on Earth began.

Remember, God said, "But of the tree of the knowledge of good and evil you shall not eat, for in the day that you eat of it you shall surely die" (Genesis 2:17). When they ate of it, they experienced the promised consequence, and the long shadow of death fell over the human race.

Another part of this curse was multiplied pain at childbirth: "To the woman He said: 'I will greatly multiply your sorrow and your conception; in pain you shall bring forth children'" (Genesis 3:16). The wonderful joy of giving birth to a child would now be impacted and overshadowed by intense physical pain.

Prior to the birth of our two boys, I went through the natural-childbirth classes with Cathe. To alleviate the pain of contractions, she practiced her breathing techniques; I was her "coach." She did a great job bringing our sons into this world. But she also went through all of the pain.

Let me just say that I'm thankful this part of the curse didn't fall on men! I would never have held up as well as she did. We men, however, also have our part of the curse to bear, which is strenuous work. Prior to his fall into sin, Adam's job was primarily to enjoy the glory and splendor of what God had made. But now he would have to labor hard and long to work and somehow scratch a living out of the earth. In Genesis 3, God said to Adam,

> *Cursed is the ground for your sake; in toil you shall eat of it all the days of your life. Both thorns and thistles it shall bring forth for you, and you shall eat the herb of the field. In the sweat of your face you shall eat bread till you return to the ground, for out of it you were taken; for dust you are, and to dust you shall return.* (vv. 3:17–19)

Strife and Selfishness

Another aspect of the curse that fell on humanity still affects our marriages to this day: strife and selfishness. After Eve sinned in the Garden—which was a result of her disobedience to God and her failure to consult with Adam about the serpent's temptation—the Lord had something very important to say to her.

He said: "Your desire shall be for your husband, and he shall rule over you" (v. 16).

When we read these words, it's important to keep in mind that *this statement was part of the curse.* Looking at the words in the original language will help us understand a dynamic that causes tension between men and women to this very day—and explains the reason for a "battle of the sexes."

The word God used for "desire" is the same one also used in Genesis 4:7—the identical Hebrew term—and comes from a root word that means "to compel, to impel, to urge, or to seek control over." Using the same word in Genesis 4:7, the Lord warned Cain, "Sin lies at the door. And its *desire* is for you, but you should rule over it" (*emphasis mine*). God was essentially saying, "Cain, sin wants to control you, but you must control sin."

In light of this close contextual meaning of the word "desire," the curse on Eve was that woman's desire would be to henceforth usurp the place of her husband's headship. In other words, she would want to rule her husband.

If you are a man reading these words, you may be thinking, *Preach it, Greg, this is good stuff! I like this.* But hold on a minute. This is a double-edged sword, because the word used in this verse for "rule" is a word that means "to subdue, to put under your feet."

This is a part of the curse, too, and it wasn't something God was advocating; rather, it was something that God was *acknowledging* as a result of sin. In other words, it was speaking of a new kind of authoritarianism that was not in God's original plan for man's headship. The distortion of woman's proper submissiveness and man's proper authority came as a direct result of Adam and Eve's sin, and the curse that followed.

This is where male chauvinism and women's liberation have their origins. Woman has a sinful inclination to usurp the authority of her husband, and man has a sinful inclination to put his wife under his feet. Both are equally wrong before God.

Equal Standing, Different Functions

Some people today assert that the Bible is a sexist book. Yet anyone who makes a statement like that demonstrates an obvious ignorance of Scripture and biblical culture. We have to examine what the Bible is really saying and dispel this ridiculous thinking.

If anything, the Bible and its message *liberated* women. The Apostle Paul, who has been wrongly labeled a chauvinist by some, said, "Husbands, love your wives, just as Christ also loved the church and gave Himself for her" (Ephesians 5:25).

Many of us have heard these words before—perhaps many times. Still, this was *revolutionary* stuff for the time in which Paul was living. Telling a husband to love his wife as Christ loved the church, to give himself for her—that was a radically different message from what husbands had heard up to that point. In Roman culture, women were treated as possessions, not partners in life. Even in the Jewish culture of the day, a man might divorce his wife for practically any reason—though he had to warp and twist Scripture to do it.

So let's not take this secular thinking of today and try to attach it to Scripture. The Bible gives us the truth about how we are to live and function.

Men and women are equal before God, but we are different. Our roles are different as well. When we fail to see that, we make a big mistake. God has wired men and women in different ways, and He uses us in different ways. Instead of being upset about it, we should celebrate it and rejoice in it, because it all works out in His plan and His balance.

Self: The Intractable Enemy of Marital Harmony

The problem with most marriages today is not money, careers, sex, children, in-laws or any of those typical reasons people give.

No, it really boils down to one word.

Self.

We love to blame this thing or that thing for our marital difficulties, but the real problem looks back at us in the mirror.

James asks, "What is causing the quarrels and fights among you? Isn't it the whole army of evil desires at war within you?" (James 4:1, NLT)

We could complain and vent for hours about one issue or another in our marriage, but here's the hard truth: We bring these problems into our marriages because of our sinful bent and our natural orientation toward pleasing ourselves.

Of course, no one would ever actually say it that way. Instead we hear the same inane, tired phrases—so devoid of real content and so terribly destructive.

"I'm no longer happy in my marriage."

"I need some time for me."

"I need my own space."

"My wife/husband is no longer meeting my needs."

"I'm going to go find myself."

It's this ridiculous, selfish orientation that destroys so many marriages, homes, and families—with reverberations that roll on for generations.

Where Strength Comes From

While it's true that selfishness is part of human nature, it is not true that we're beyond the hope of changing. The Bible tells us, "If anyone is in Christ, he is a new creation; old things have passed away; behold, all things have become new" (2 Corinthians 5:17). God is telling us that we have a new nature, and that we are to live by new standards.

But here's the best part: He has given us new power to accomplish those very things.

Questions for Discussion

1. *"If you are angry, don't sin by nursing your grudge. Don't let the sun go down with you still angry—get over it quickly; for when you are angry, you give a mighty foothold to the devil"* (Ephesians 4:26-27, TLB).

What do you think it means to give the devil a "mighty foothold" in your marriage? In addition to unresolved anger, what are some other such footholds that Satan might try to exploit to damage the closeness between a husband and wife?

Anger, misunderstanding, fress?netion

2. The right motive for marriage, this chapter says, is to make your *mate* happy, meet your *mate's* needs, and bring your *mate* fulfillment. How does this advice go against the grain of what our culture advocates? How can we keep from being influenced by the culture's unending "me-first" emphasis?

Cultures me]st

3. The chapter says: *"Activists do everything in their power to undermine and redefine what marriage and family really are. Using the tools of humor and cynicism, novelists, songwriters, and TV- and movie-writers deliberately mock and ridicule traditional roles, values and families."*

If this is the sort of message we keep getting over and over again through our culture's media, does it make sense to limit some forms of that media in our lives? Why or why not?

Yes it does Wi because what we think.

4. The first part of 2 Timothy 3:1-2 tells us, "In the last days perilous times will come: For men will be *lovers of themselves…*"

What evidence do you see of this being played out in today's world? What makes these times "perilous" for marriages and families?

[handwritten: selfishness, not being thoughtful, expecting others to fill no want of filling them]

5. *"Let nothing be done through selfish ambition or conceit, but in lowliness of mind let each* esteem others *better than himself. Let each of you look out not only for his own interests, but also for the interests of others"* (Philippians 2:3–4).

Our culture tells us that we don't have enough self-love, and that one of our biggest needs is for self-confidence, self-esteem, self-worth and self-expression. How much truth is there to these assertions? How do we balance healthy self-esteem with the Bible's teaching to put God and others before our own needs and desires?

[handwritten: confidence in being God's or is good. our confidence that we can do it on our own are dangerous]

6. Romans 12:2 (PHILLIPS) reads, *"Don't let the world around you squeeze you into its own mould, but let God re-mould your minds from within, so that you may prove in practice that the plan of God for you is good, meets all his demands and moves towards the goal of true maturity."*

Applying this verse to our marriages, describe the tension between the world seeking to mold us from the outside in, and God seeking to re-mold us from the inside out.

7. After God confronted Adam with his disobedience and sin, Adam said, "The woman whom You gave to be with me, she gave me of the tree, and I ate" (v. 12). Greg calls this the world's first lame excuse. And Eve essentially said, "The devil made me do it." In what ways do we continue this trend of blaming "someone else" for our marriage difficulties, rather than facing up to hard truths about ourselves?

8. Greg writes: *"Men and women are equal before God, but we are different. Our roles are different as well. When we fail to see that, we make a big mistake. God has wired men and women in different ways, and He uses us in different ways. Instead of being upset about it, we should celebrate it and rejoice in it, because it all works out in His plan and His balance."*

Describe some examples you can think of when this God-ordained balance between the roles and the strengths and weaknesses of the sexes has worked out very well. What happens when we refuse to acknowledge that men and women are equal but *different*?

9. Greg writes: *"We could complain and vent for hours about one issue or another in our marriage, but here's the hard truth: We bring these problems into our marriages because of our sinful bent and our natural orientation toward pleasing ourselves."*

To what extent do you agree or disagree with this statement? If you agree that this is true, what can you and your spouse do about it?

CHAPTER 4

Heart Preparation

As children copy their fathers you, as God's children, are to copy him.
Live your lives in love—the same sort of love which Christ gives us and
which he perfectly expressed when he gave himself up for us in sacrifice
to God. –Ephesians 5:1-2, PHILLIPS

I heard about a husband and wife who were celebrating their 25th wedding anniversary.

Taking his wife by the hands, the husband made a dramatic announcement: "Dear, in honor of our 25 years of wedded bliss, I have decided to take you to China."

"China!" she said, amazed and touched. "I've never been to China. I'm so excited. Wow…if you're doing something this extravagant for our 25th, what will you do for our 50th?"

"That's when I'll pick you up," he replied.

That might be *someone's* idea of a good marriage, but not mine! And it's not God's, either. The Bible tells me, "You husbands likewise, live with your wives in an understanding way…"[13]

That's God's way, and God's way is the only way I want for something as precious and valuable to me as my marriage.

By saying that, I'm also saying that I *don't* want marriage the world's way. The world—and by that I mean our culture—is largely hostile toward the family and everything it stands for. I have never known a time when the family is under attack as it is today from those who not only want to undermine it, but to even redefine it.

The good news is this: We don't have to rely on our culture's constantly morphing definition of marriage and family, no matter how dominant and insistent that voice might become in movies, TV and media. We don't have to look for secular advice on how to succeed in marriage—and life.

We have something *far* better.

We have the eternal, unchanging, utterly reliable Word of God.

The Bible speaks directly to men and women and tells us how to have a happy and successful marriage.

When the day came for me to stand at the altar with Cathe, I knew I was making a lifelong commitment. And with the grace and help of God, it was a commitment I would honor and keep. When I said those vows, I *meant* them. And so did she.

In this chapter, we'll consider what God has to say about marriage. But not just any ordinary, plain-vanilla, garden-variety marriage. We will look at His plan for a marriage that is both blessed and successful.

In other words, just a little bit of heaven on earth.

"God's Solid Foundation"

The Word of God doesn't just give us beautiful language or lofty ideals. No, the Bible is *alive* with truth—truth that works and changes and transforms lives. It also changes marriages. I've seen it happen more times than I can count.

But sometimes people don't like or appreciate what the Bible teaches about the role of the husband and the wife. In fact, it runs directly counter to strong opinions in today's culture. Nevertheless, it is the Word of God; it's true and it stands no matter how the culture shifts and changes all around it.

As Paul said to Timothy, "Nevertheless, God's solid foundation stands firm."[10] And so it does, to this very day.

Sometimes when people come to me for marriage counseling, it means they've tried everything else, and this is the last resort. By the time they think of coming to "talk to the pastor," their relationship may be hanging by a thread.

When I sit down with a couple for our initial counseling session, the first question I ask is if they're both Christians. They usually say yes. Then I ask them if they both believe the Bible is the Word of God. Again, they usually reply in the affirmative.

But *then* I ask them, "Are you willing to do what the Bible says, even if you find it difficult?"

That's when the hesitation begins. They shoot each other glances and realize that if they say yes, they'll be stepping into my trap. Even so, it's an all-important question for that couple—or any couple. Why? *Because I have never found a couple contemplating divorce who were truly doing what the Word of God says they should do in their marriage.* What's more, I don't think I ever will. If a husband and wife are willing in their hearts to roll up their sleeves and actually do what God says, they won't have to worry about divorce court in their future. But if they reject, water-down, or compromise the Bible's clear principles, they will find trouble up ahead.

Divorce, of course has become commonplace—and almost casual—in contemporary society. It's bad enough when you observe that in our culture as a whole, but when you see it happening in the church of Jesus Christ, that's cause for grave concern. Yet that is the very tragedy we're seeing today across our country. We're seeing men and women who profess to be followers of Jesus Christ, yet simply disregard what the Word of God says about marriage.

As I've said, most divorces I've witnessed could have been avoided, but the husband and wife just don't want to follow through on the biblical principles that would save their marriage. Yes, there are biblical grounds for a divorce, such as infidelity, but most divorces I've seen are not for biblical reasons. It's more a matter of two people who can't seem to get along anymore, or a general disappointment and unhappiness that poisons the most important human relationship in life. And so they passively let the relationship go, in the vague hope that "something else will work out."

That is not God's way. He intended the marriage relationship to be permanent. In my view, *wedlock* equals *padlock*. If that sounds "confining" to you, it's actually not. It is incredibly liberating, as we will see in the chapters to come.

Some of the best marriage counsel in the Bible can be found in the fifth chapter of Paul's letter to the church at Ephesus, and we will explore those verses in detail. But before the apostle starts giving specific advice for wives and husbands, he does a little vision-casting. He shows us how to prepare our lives in order to become the best marriage partner we can be.

The View From Ephesians 5

Sometimes when you walk into a really nice restaurant or a beautiful home, you're immediately struck by the view. Perhaps the first thing you see as you enter through front door are large windows with a panoramic view of the ocean, the mountains, the city lights, or some other striking scene.

It's so inviting. It's the kind of room where you want to linger.

So it is when you walk through the "doorway" of Ephesians 5. The view of marriage from this chapter elevates the relationship of husband and wife to amazing new heights. It's living truth, strong truth, and it is also beautiful.

Before he addresses the specifics of marriage, though, the Apostle Paul gets down to the nitty-gritty in this section of his letter, dealing with issues and temptations we face even as Christians. He begins by telling them, "Be imitators of God as dear children."

Therefore be imitators of God as dear children. And walk in love, as Christ also has loved us and given Himself for us, an offering and a sacrifice to God for a sweet-smelling aroma.

But fornication and all uncleanness or covetousness, let it not even be named among you, as is fitting for saints; neither filthiness, nor foolish talking, nor coarse jesting, which are not fitting, but rather giving of thanks. For this you know, that no fornicator, unclean person, nor covetous man, who is an idolater, has any inheritance in the kingdom of Christ and God. Let no one deceive you with empty words, for because of these things the wrath of God comes upon the sons of disobedience. Therefore do not be partakers with them.

For you were once darkness, but now you are light in the Lord.
Walk as children of light (for the fruit of the Spirit is in all
goodness, righteousness, and truth), finding out what is acceptable
to the Lord. And have no fellowship with the unfruitful works of
darkness, but rather expose them. For it is shameful even to speak
of those things which are done by them in secret.
(Ephesians 5:1-12)

"Dear children." That's a nice phrase. The fact is, you aren't
simply a child of God; you are a dear—beloved—child of God.
Do you realize how much God loves you? Are you aware of the
depth of His affection toward you?

When the Lord Jesus was baptized by John, the Father spoke
from heaven and said, "You are My beloved Son; in You I am
well pleased."[11]

We know that God the Father was very pleased with His Son.
God loved and loves His Son, the Lord Jesus Christ.

"That's great," you say. "But that's Jesus. That's not me." But
listen to these amazing words that Jesus uttered in His prayer in
the Gospel of John. He said:

I have given them the glory you gave me, so that they may be one,
as we are—I in them and you in me, all being perfected into one.
Then the world will know that you sent me and will understand
that you love them as much as you love me.
(John 17:22-23, NIV, emphasis mine)

What? Could that really be true?

Jesus just said that God the Father loves me as much as He
loves Jesus Christ! If the Lord Himself hadn't said it, I wouldn't
dare even to suggest such a thing. Yet this is exactly what the
Bible teaches. You are a dear and deeply loved son or daughter
of God.

So…let's start *living* that way.

So many times you and I don't behave like dearly loved,
highly valued children of the living God. But that's precisely what
we are. We have been adopted into His family with full rights
and privileges. The Bible says that when we become believers in
Jesus, we are "accepted in the Beloved."[12] And that simply means
that now God sees you in His Son, Jesus Christ. He doesn't see

you for what you were; He sees you for what you are—and what He will make you into!

How should the knowledge that we are accepted in this way by God—that we are His dear children—affect me in the way I live in this world? In several ways.

First, it should help me to avoid immorality.

Ephesians 5:3 says: "But fornication and all uncleanness or covetousness, let it not even be named among you, as is fitting for saints."

Now why would Paul bring up such unsavory topics like these? It helps to understand the situation these believers lived in at that time. Ephesus was the capital of the Roman province of Asia, a busy and affluent commercial port. But it was also cult headquarters for the goddess Diana.

Immorality was rampant throughout the city. Thousands of prostitutes working for the temple would comb the streets of the city, looking for potential recruits. They would lure men into the temple to engage in sexual rites as they offered worship to this false deity.

So these Ephesian believers were godly people living in a godless place. Paul told them, in effect, "I want to just spell it out for you guys. As followers of Jesus, you can't live a compromised lifestyle. No more of this!"

Is this an appropriate word for today's culture? You'd better believe it. We too are sex obsessed, and bombarded on all sides with invitations to immorality.

What is "fornication"? It is sex outside of marriage, and there is never any justification, rationale or "special allowance" for that. It is *always* a sin before God.

But Paul doesn't just mention that. He also mentions "uncleanness" and "covetousness," saying that we shouldn't allow even a *hint* of these things in our lives. Not a hint! That's very important. This, I believe, speaks to our electronic culture. We may not (technically) be engaging in extramarital sex, doing the twisted things that wicked people do, but we can *watch* them do these things on our TVs, computers and smartphones. In the sick, voyeuristic world we live in today, we can follow the latest antics of godless actors and entertainers who post their activities on YouTube or Twitter. I have never seen so much interest in the lifestyles of these so-called celebrities like we see today.

And what does Paul say about it? He says you are an imitator of God, and a treasured child of God. Not only should you not do those things, but there shouldn't even be hint of this stuff in your life.

Then he takes it a step further.

Second, it should motivate me to avoid obscene talk.

Look at verse 4: "Neither filthiness, nor foolish talking, nor coarse jesting, which are not fitting, but rather giving of thanks."

"Filthiness" has to do with general obscenity—talk that is disgraceful and degrading. Paul also mentions coarse jesting, which covers the double entendre and sexual innuendo. Some people can turn anything into a weird joke. They begin to see everything through the lens of sexual obsession, and distort innocent remarks into off-color "humor." In other words, their minds and hearts are so full of their obsessions that it colors their life and their speech.

Paul says, "No! it should not be that way among God's children."

And it most certainly shouldn't be that way among pastors, who are specifically called to be examples to the flock (1 Peter 5:3).

Strange as it may seem, there's a popular trend in some churches today for pastors to use obscene language in the pulpit. Some think that sort of thing is "daring" or "relevant" or "authentic."

No, it's just plain wrong.

If that's what I as a pastor would have to do to be relevant, then I will be irrelevant. The fact is, you can be authentic without crossing the line of decency. You can be down-to-earth without being "earthy."

There is also a trend in some churches today to use an emphasis on sex to attract crowds. They will teach through the book of

Song of Solomon, which is fine, because it's a book in the Bible and inspired by God. But they will teach it as though it was some kind of explicit sex manual, instead of presenting it with respect, delicacy and honor. In this way, these teachers play to the epicurean interests of a twisted culture. And all of this is done in the name of "re-envisioning" or "re-imagining" church.

We don't need to do that.

We don't need to re-envision or re-imagine church. We need to rediscover it the way God gave it to us in the Bible.

Third, it should motivate me to avoid coveting.

Verse 5 tells us: "For this you know, that no fornicator, unclean person, nor covetous man, who is an idolater, has any inheritance in the kingdom of Christ and God."

What is coveting? You could actually translate the word "covet" to "pant after." Picture a thirsty animal with its tongue hanging out. That's the concept here, and it isn't very attractive. To covet is to eagerly desire or set your heart on something (or someone) that belongs to another. It might be your neighbor's wife or husband, or it might be something they own that you don't.

Paul tells them, "That sort of attitude doesn't belong in one of God's sons or daughters."

Fourth, it should encourage me to walk in a new way.

In verses 8-10 we read: "For you were once darkness, but now you are light in the Lord. Walk as children of light (for the fruit of the Spirit is in all goodness, righteousness, and truth), finding out what is acceptable to the Lord."

Paul uses three words to describe how we are to walk as believers: in *goodness*, in *righteousness*, and in *truth*.

How should we walk? In *goodness*.

A better translation of the word would be "generosity." Godly people should be generous people, not stingy.

How should we walk? In *righteousness*.

In this context, this speaks of integrity in our dealings with others. Christians should be godly and aboveboard in all their business dealings. You can't shrug and say, "Well, business is business." That may very well be the same as saying, "Hey, I'll do whatever it takes to get ahead in my particular line of work." It's good to excel in our jobs or professions, and to succeed to the best of our ability. But we also need to do our work with honesty and integrity.

How should we walk? In *truth*.

This means an absence of falsehood and deception. Godly people should be honest people. But that's not all. Godly people have yet another obligation.

Fifth, it should embolden me to confront sin.

Verse 11 says, "Have no fellowship with the unfruitful works of darkness, but rather expose them." This gets tricky now, because the watchwords of our day are tolerance, acceptance and understanding. According to our contemporary culture, there is no higher value than "tolerance."

Sometimes in the course of teaching the Bible, I'll highlight a particular teaching that's making the rounds in our country, and I will say, "According to the Bible, this teaching is wrong."

Occasionally someone will tell me, "Pastor Greg, what you said wasn't loving."

But it *is* loving. As a shepherd, I'm seeking to protect God's people from a teaching or direction that could harm them. How is that not loving? It would be like seeing a wolf sneak through a hole in the fence while your toddler plays in the backyard, and you drive that wolf away with a stick.

Is that "loving"?

Well, maybe not for the wolf. But it is for the child!

For the sake of a little one, I would repel that predator with harsh measures, and do so without a pang of conscience. In the same way, we have to confront sin when we see it.

But don't expect to win any popularity contests for doing that. If you speak out for what is true, you will quickly be branded as intolerant, bigoted, puritanical and narrow. Be that as it may, the Bible tells us, "Have no fellowship with the unfruitful works of darkness, but expose them." To *expose* carries the idea of reproof, correction, punishment or discipline. It is to confront sin. So if you have a friend who claims to be a follower of Jesus, and you see him or her making serious moral compromises, you need to confront that friend.

Just make sure you do so with love and wisdom.

We all know people who feel it's their job to be professional confronters, and are just a little too quick on the draw to condemn everything. At the same time, however, there are many more people who are so reticent and passive that they never face up to evil at all, and refuse to deal with anything.

Scripture gives us a great model in the person of Nathan the prophet. King David had fallen into sin, committing adultery with Bathsheba and then arranging for her husband's death in battle. He had not repented of those sins, and he lived like that for a full year.

Nathan bided his time, waiting for the right moment to approach the king. Finally, he told David a story about a stolen lamb, and the king took the bait, proclaiming that the heartless, selfish individual who stole that little lamb deserved to die. Nathan looked David right in the eyes and boldly said, "*You* are the man."

Nathan knew very well the king could have had his head for that confrontation. But the godly prophet must have said in his heart, "So be it. I can't allow my friend to go on living a lie, and in rebellion against God." So he spoke up, in spite of the risk.

When we confront someone, we must go in humility and love, speaking the truth to those who need to hear it. That's what God's Word is telling us. Paul wraps up these words with an exhortation to walk in wisdom, joy and gratitude, before he turns to husbands and wives with specific direction (as we will see in the pages to come).

But all things that are exposed are made manifest by the light, for whatever makes manifest is light. Therefore He says:

"Awake, you who sleep,

Arise from the dead,
And Christ will give you light."

See then that you walk circumspectly, not as fools but as wise,
redeeming the time, because the days are evil.

Therefore do not be unwise, but understand what the will of the
Lord is. And do not be drunk with wine, in which is dissipation;
but be filled with the Spirit, speaking to one another in psalms and
hymns and spiritual songs, singing and making melody in your
heart to the Lord, giving thanks always for all things to God the
Father in the name of our Lord Jesus Christ, submitting to one
another in the fear of God. (Ephesians 5:13-21)

Turn on the Light

Verse 13: "All things … are made manifest by the light … whatever makes manifest is light."

Did you ever misplace anything in the dark? How do you find it again, unless you turn on the light? Sometimes when I'm getting ready in the morning, I'll dress in the dark so I don't disturb my wife. But then when I get out into the light, I see what I have on and realize, "Oh…this doesn't exactly match, does it?"

Light illuminates. Light reveals. Light shows things for what they really are. So shine the light of God's Word on your life and your marriage—or on your single life, for that matter. The Bible says, "Wake up and turn on the light. Life is too short to sleepwalk through your days."

Wake up

Verse 14: "Awake, you who sleep…"

In other words, get the sleep out of your eyes and the fog out of your mind. Be alert. Take action. Wake up to the reality of a culture that is hostile to the family and to your faith.

Walk carefully

Verse 15 says: "Walk circumspectly…"

This word speaks of something that is accurate and exact. It conveys the idea of examining or investigating something with great care. It's attention to detail. It reminds me of preparing to sign an important contract or document—you want to be sure you read the fine print before you sign your John Hancock on the dotted line.

In the same way, if you want to have a successful marriage, read the fine print of what God's Word says. Don't say your vows until you're truly ready to live by them. Successful marriages aren't obtained by careless, random or haphazard living. No, good marriages result when husbands and wives pay attention to detail, and carefully apply biblical principles to their lives. To be the husband, wife, father or mother God wants us to be, we must acknowledge our profound need of God's help—His strength, perspective, wisdom and grace.

Redeem the time.

Verse 16 says "…redeeming the time, because the days are evil." The Phillips translation renders the verse as follows: *"Make the best use of your time, despite all the difficulties of these days."*

In other words, avoid frittering away your hours and days on worthless pursuits. Get your house in order, and get your life sorted out. As the prophet said to King Hezekiah, "Thus says the LORD: 'Set your house in order, for you shall die and not live'" (Isaiah 38:1).

When you think about it, that's true of all of us.

Each one of us will live out our brief lives on Earth, and then stand before our Creator. Is your house in order? Is it what God wants it to be?

You say, "Greg, it isn't easy to be a husband…or a wife…or a parent." That's true. But God will never ask you to do anything without providing you with the power to do so.

Be Filled With the Holy Spirit

Verse 18 reads: "Don't be drunk with wine, but be filled with the Spirit."

In the verses following the passage above, we read that wives are to submit to their husbands, and husbands are to love their wives as Christ loved the church. But before a word is spoken about any of these things, God says, "Be filled with the Spirit."

Why?

Because we can't live an unselfish life or become an other-centered spouse apart from the direct empowerment of God's Holy Spirit. A husband cannot love his wife as Christ loves the church, and a wife cannot effectively submit to her husband as unto the Lord, without supernatural help and enabling.

Before a word is ever mentioned about the specific roles of the husband and wife in this vital chapter of Ephesians, God puts forth His prerequisite: "Be filled with the Spirit." In the original language, this statement is a command. God isn't saying, "Would you mind, as a personal favor to Me, if you have time, please, be filled with the Spirit." No, God is saying, "I command you to be filled with the Spirit."

There's another thing we need to know about the phrase "be filled with the Spirit." It speaks of a continuous action. It could be translated from the Greek as "be constantly filled over and over again with the Holy Spirit."

Say you went out and bought a new car. You were told this car would run 100,000 miles, easy—maybe 200,000. *That's great*, you think. So you drive it off the lot, and run around town on your new wheels for a week or so with no problems. Then one day, it sputters and comes to a standstill. *That salesperson lied to me*, you say to yourself. Then on your dashboard you notice a little red light and an arrow pointing to the letter E.

You're out of fuel. You don't need to take the car back and trade it in, and you don't need a new engine. You just need to go to a gas station and get a refill.

In the same way, your marriage can be humming along, things going great. Then all of the sudden, you find yourself chugging rather than humming. Maybe you've found yourself thinking, *It's my spouse. He/she isn't meeting my needs anymore. I think we've fallen out of love. I guess I need to trade this old model in for a new one.*

No. You just need a refill.

Did you know that God gives refills?

There's nothing complicated about it. You just pull in and say, "Lord, fill me with Your wonderful Holy Spirit. Fill me again." Each and every day you say, "Lord, I need to be empowered by and filled with Your Spirit. I am completely dependent upon You."

This command speaks to life in its totality. But it also applies to the marriage relationship in particular. If you want to be the husband or wife God wants you to be, you need the power of the Holy Spirit in your life.

But what exactly does it mean to be "filled with the Holy Spirit"?

Under His Control

The first thing we should note is that in the Greek, this verb "be filled" is in the imperative mode. What does that mean? It means we're talking about a command, not a suggestion! To fail to do so is to effectively cut off your power supply, and render you unable to be the spouse or parent God intends.

The verb in the Greek also speaks of a continuous action. A better translation would be, "Be *continuously* filled with the Holy Spirit." Let me add here that this may having nothing to do with your emotions. Many of us attach way too much emotional baggage to the filling of the Spirit. You don't have to weep and wail, tremble and shake, or even raise your voice. That's not what it means to be filled. Another way you could translate "be filled" is *"be controlled"* by the Spirit.

The Greek word speaks of wind filling a sail. So there you are in your little sailboat out on a lake, and a gust of wind comes, filling your sails and moving you forward toward the desired destination.

I love that imagery. There is power, beauty and practicality in that picture of a wind-filled sail thrusting a boat forward through the waves. In the same way, God's Spirit wants to empower us, move us, guide us and direct us.

But that Greek term translated "filled" could also mean "to permeate." It's the idea of salt permeating meat. Back when the

New Testament was written, meat was preserved was by rubbing salt deep into its fibers. This tells us that the Holy Spirit wants to permeate our lives, touching everything we think, do, and say, entering every fiber of our being.

So let the Holy Spirit fill your sails. Let the Holy Spirit permeate every area of your life. Let the Holy Spirit control you in all that you say and do. This is a clear command, and something you should do over and over again.

If you do, you'll have the strongest help in all the universe to be the husband or wife that God—and your spouse—most deeply desires.

"Submitting to One Another..."

With all of these practical words of counsel and instruction as a backdrop, Paul turns to the particular issue of marriage, and the relationship between a husband and a wife.

> ...submitting to one another in the fear of God.

> Wives, submit to your own husbands, as to the Lord. For the husband is head of the wife, as also Christ is head of the church; and He is the Savior of the body. Therefore, just as the church is subject to Christ, so let the wives be to their own husbands in everything. (vv. 21-24)

Let's start with an unpopular word in our culture—a word that very few people like to hear in any context. The word is *submission*.

We don't like the idea of submitting, do we? And yet this is a word that surfaces again and again in the pages of the Bible.

Why are we afraid to submit? Some might say, "Because I don't want anyone taking advantage of me. I have my rights, and I ought to have my say-so the same as anyone else."

So when someone quotes Ephesians 5:21, about wives submitting to husbands, you will have people who say, "I don't agree with that."

But hold on. Let's first make sure we actually understand what this verse means. In the previous verse we read, "...submitting to one another in the fear of God." Then, after setting that context, we read:

> *Wives, submit to your own husbands, as to the Lord. For the husband is head of the wife, as also Christ is head of the church; and He is the Savior of the body. Therefore, just as the church is subject to Christ, so let the wives be to their own husbands in everything. (vv. 22-24)*

Mutual Submission

Not only, then, are wives to submit to husbands, but *husbands are to submit to their wives as well*. Why? Because the first command here is "honor Christ by submitting to each other" (TLB).

What does this actually mean? To submit means to get in order under something. It's sometimes used in a military sense and means "to rank beneath." For instance, in the military you have different ranks—general, colonel, first lieutenant, and so forth. There is a chain of command in the military, and a chain of command in life as well.

So here's what this passage is saying. A husband's submission to his wife does not mean he abdicates his responsibility of leadership in the home. But it *does* mean that it helps her to bear her burdens. You could also translate this verse as "supporting one another in the fear of God." He gets underneath her to help carry her cares, and remains ready to sacrifice his own desires and meet her needs. And she is willing to do the same for him.

Another way to say it? *Put the needs of your mate above your own.*

Imagine a married person saying something like this: "I want this marriage to be about my spouse, not about me. I want to make my wife the happiest woman who ever lived." Or, "I want to make my husband the happiest man in the world." Do you know how much that sort of mindset would change your marriage?

No, that isn't "natural" to us.

If fact, it's supernatural.

It takes the power and presence of God to accomplish it. Paul tells us to imitate God and walk in love, but we need the indwelling presence of the Holy Spirit enabling us to follow that path day by day, moment by moment.

Far too often we make marriage about me and my needs. *How can she fulfill me? How can he make me a happier person? What can he/she do for me?*

These days we see all sorts of TV ads for computer match-making programs, offering assistance to people who hope to find the right person. *A successful marriage, however, isn't so much about finding the right person as much as it is about BEING the right person.*

There is no perfect person out there, no matter how many identical boxes both of you might check on some online survey. It's about you being willing to change and adapt for the sake of your spouse. Philippians 2:4-6 (TLB) says:

> *Don't think only about your own affairs, but be interested in others, too, and what they are doing. Your attitude should be the same that Christ Jesus had. Though he was God, he did not demand and cling to his rights as God.*

Another Scripture that undergirds the idea of mutual submission is 1 Corinthians 7:3-4 (NLT), where the Apostle Paul is speaking about sexual relations. He writes:

> *The husband should not deprive his wife of sexual intimacy, which is her right as a married woman, nor should the wife deprive her husband. The wife gives authority over her body to her husband, and the husband also gives authority over his body to his wife.*

Do you see Paul's point here? The husband no more possesses his wife than she possesses him. He is not superior; she is not inferior. And vice versa. *They belong one to another.* Paul is saying, "Her body belongs to you, and your body belongs to her. So don't deprive each other sexually unless you have agreed to this for a specific purpose and for a limited amount of time."

Here, once again, is the kernel of this teaching: You belong to one another. You support one another. You submit to one another. You help one another. *The two of you have become one.* In no way does the Bible teach that man is better than woman, or even above woman. We stand before God on equal ground. Galatians 3:28 says that in Christ "there is neither Jew nor Greek, slave nor free, male nor female." We are one in Jesus.

But even though there is no difference between man and woman in the nature of their salvation or standing with God, there is a principle of authority in the family. Those who struggle with the concept of the husband being the head of the home might be helped by considering Paul's words in 1 Corinthians 11:3 (NIV)…

> *I want you to realize that the head of every man is Christ, and the head of the woman is man, and the head of Christ is God.*

What does it mean that "the head of Christ is God"? The Bible speaks of a Trinity—Father, Son and Holy Spirit. One is not better than the other. They are the same in nature and essence. At the same time, however, we read in Scripture that the Son submits to the Father—and not because the Son is in any sense less than the Father. We see this played out beautifully in the Lord's life on Earth, where He constantly submitted to the Father, called on the Father and prayed to the Father. Yet Jesus Christ is Himself God incarnate, and the Holy Spirit is God as well.

Paul, then, is saying that the relationship structure of Jesus Christ to God the Father is the same as the relationship structure in marriage. Though the husband and wife are equal in their standing before God, in order for the family to function in harmony, the woman (with no loss of dignity) takes a place of submission to the leadership of her husband. God's divine design intends that her respect, help and obedience will be matched by his servant leadership as they submit together to the Lord Jesus Christ and to each other.

Any guy with half a brain knows that marriage is a *partnership*, and he doesn't try to run the home like a banana-republic dictator. That's not what it means to lead. Biblical leadership is servant leadership. It is to lead as Jesus led.

If a man has to beat his chest and yell, "I am the head of this home, and you do what I tell you to do," something is very, very wrong. If he has true authority, he won't have to resort to screaming and pounding on walls.

No, he will have his wife's love and respect—and his leader-ship will be a natural result.

Questions for Discussion

1. Greg contrasts an "ordinary, plain-vanilla, garden-variety marriage" with a marriage that is both blessed and successful. In fact, "just a little bit of heaven on earth."

The longer you live, the more you realize how quickly life flies by. All too soon, life will be behind us, and we'll be looking back. What are some ways we can lift our marriage relationship above the "ordinary, plain-vanilla" level and make it something special?

Based on the Bible - respect each other

2. Reflecting on decades of experience in ministry, Greg Laurie writes: *"If a husband and wife are willing in their hearts to roll up their sleeves and actually do what God says, they won't have to worry about divorce court in their future. But if they reject, water-down, or compromise the Bible's clear principles, they will find trouble up ahead."*

What would be an example of "watering down" or compromising the Bible's principles on marriage?

3. Greg writes: *"Most divorces I've seen are not for biblical reasons. It's more a matter of two people who can't seem to get along anymore, or a general disappointment and unhappiness that poisons the most important human relationship in life. And so they passively let the relationship go, in the vague hope that 'something else will work out.'"*

Does this statement match up with what you have seen of divorce in your experience? What are the negative, destructive attitudes that Greg lists here, and how (with God's help) might they be countered? *selfish mecontinued*

Lazy bored

4. God intended the marriage relationship to be permanent. *"Wedlock equals padlock."* Does that sound confining or liberating to you? Explain your answer.

No that's what it should be stable trustworthy

5. Review John 17:22-23. If you were able to really get a grip on the fact that God loves you as much as He loves His own Son, Jesus, what difference would that make in your life? How might it impact our insecurities or fears?

Confidence + trust that you are loved

6. How could knowing that you are a dearly loved son or daughter of God keep you from immorality…obscene language…and coveting what doesn't belong to you?

trust + believe that Gods plan is perfect

7. Ephesians 5:11 says, *"Have no fellowship with the unfruitful works of darkness, but rather expose them."* How do we handle a biblical directive like this in a culture that seems to value "tolerance" above all else?

Be careful not to get sucked in, walk your own path confidently

8. Greg writes: *"To expose carries the idea of reproof, correction, punishment or discipline. It is to confront sin. So if you have a friend who claims to be a follower of Jesus, and you see him or her making serious moral compromises, you need to confront that friend. Just make sure you do so with love and wisdom."*

What risks do we run when we attempt to lovingly confront sin in someone we care about? What risks do we run if we keep silent? How do we balance those risks?

lose a friend   lose respect   that's tough

9. Quoting Ephesians 5:14, "Awake, you who sleep," Greg counsels to *"get the sleep out of your eyes and the fog out of your mind. Be alert. Take action. Wake up to the reality of a culture that is hostile to the family and your faith."*

What causes that spiritual sleepiness and fog to come into our lives? What are its dangers? What steps can we take to be more alert to both the dangers and opportunities confronting our families?

10. The Phillips translation of Ephesians 5:16 says, *"Make the best use of your time, despite all the difficulties of these days."* Recognizing the danger to even Christian marriages and families today, what steps can you and your spouse take to make better use of your available time?

CHAPTER 5
Submitting...to Honor Christ

Honor Christ by submitting to each other. –Ephesians 5:21, TLB

When Mattel first introduced Teen Talk Barbie some years ago, one of her many phrases triggered a great public outcry. Four little words generated such a public-relations dilemma for Mattel that "Teen Talk Barbie" had to be yanked from the market until she changed her tune. The offending remark?

"Math class is tough!"

If *Ken* had said that, probably no one would have even noticed. But as this Barbie inadvertently confirmed, there is a hypersensitivity in our culture regarding what a woman is—or is not.

If ever there were a concept relating to women that was unpopular today, it would be the one we're about to look at in Scripture. Many would say the concepts found in the pages of the New Testament are outdated and archaic in our now-liberated society. Yes, they are old-fashioned to some, but to others, they're right on the cutting edge of life.

More importantly, biblical concepts and principles actually work in life. God's Word always makes a difference when it is heeded and applied. Why? Quite simply, because it's *true*.

As we look at the state of the American family in the 21st century, we can safely say that very reason it's falling apart is because we have strayed from God's standards.

Not only have we strayed from the standards, but they are

now openly mocked, belittled and scorned.

I firmly believe the breakdown of the family can, to a great degree, be laid at the feet of men today, because the role of the man in the home is that of initiator and leader. Because men have largely failed to fulfill this responsibility God has given them, we see the ripple effects in the home, in wives, in children, and in the society as a whole.

A Christian woman reading these words might readily nod her head, saying, "Yes, that's true. It's the failure of the men."

But that conclusion will only take you so far, because marriage is a two-way street. While men have their part in the relationship, which God has clearly laid out in Scripture, God also calls His daughters to specific standards.

And one of those standards is to submit to the leadership of her husband, as unto the Lord.

#1: The Motive of Submission

How is a woman to submit to her husband? Ephesians 5:22 says, "Wives, submit to your own husbands, *as to the Lord*." In other words, they submit to their husband as an act of submission to Jesus Christ Himself. Colossians 3:23 (NIV) says, "Whatever you do, work at it with all your heart, as working for the Lord, not for men." Whatever you do, do it for the Lord, and as unto Him.

I remember years ago visiting in the home of Billy and Ruth Graham. Ruth, now with the Lord, was a wonderful woman of God—and one of the most fun-loving people I've ever met. She was quick to laugh with a twinkle in her eye, but a true student of the Bible as well.

The day we visited, Ruth made lunch for us, and then washed the dishes by hand. I couldn't help noticing the sign over her sink that read: "Divine service done here three times a day." I was so impressed by that; she did even the small tasks of life as unto the Lord.

And so can you and I!

You can do anything "as unto the Lord." Whether you're a

doctor, songwriter, gardener or a hamburger flipper, "Whatever you do, put your whole heart and soul into it, as into work done for God, and not merely for men" (Colossians 3:23, PHILLIPS).

I think that's the heart of this instruction to wives. Submit as unto Jesus Christ. Do it for Him, in honor and reverence of Him and His place in your life. If you have difficulty submitting to your husband, then submit to God's Son, who loves you and died for you. Don't just do it for your husband—do it as though Jesus Himself asked it of you.

#2: The Model of Submission

In Ephesians 5:23-24 we read: "For the husband is head of the wife, as also Christ is head of the church; and He is the Savior of the body. Therefore, just as the church is subject to Christ, so let the wives be to their own husbands in everything."

The ultimate model of submission is Jesus Christ, who laid down His privileges and rights, and ultimately His life—for us. In John 13, Jesus took off His outer garment, got down on His hands and knees, and washed the dirty feet of His disciples. He is our model.

#3: The Limits of Submission

Here's where it gets interesting. Does a Christian wife have to do everything her husband says, no matter what?

No, that's not what the Bible teaches.

A wife's submission—as a husband's—should first be to God. 1 Peter 2:13–14 (NIV) reads,

Submit yourselves for the Lord's sake to every authority instituted among men: whether to the king, as the supreme authority, or to governors, who are sent by him to punish those who do wrong and to commend those who do right.

That, of course, means I should obey the laws of the land and pay my taxes. As citizens and believers, we have to obey those laws. That's the way our country works. Authority has been instituted by God, and we must respect it. But what if that same government passed a law tomorrow that said no one can pray to

God anymore?

Daniel was presented with this exact quandary when the king of the Persian Empire signed a law that no one could pray to any god except the king himself. What did Daniel do? The Bible tells us that he continued to pray to the Lord, just as he always had. He didn't change his practice at all.

There comes a point where the law of God supersedes the law of man. What if the government passes a law that says we can't preach the Gospel anymore? Do we shut everything down? No, we go on preaching and teaching just as we always have. When the apostles were told by the authorities that they could no longer preach in the name of Jesus, they said, "We ought to obey God rather than man" (Acts 5:29).

Let's apply this principle to marriage. Say the husband is a nonbeliever, and you are the sweet, godly, Christian wife. Somehow he learns about the biblical principle of submission, and he kind of likes that idea. So he says to his wife, "Why don't you submit to me while we go out drinking tonight?" Or, "Why don't you submit to me while I ask you to do this immoral thing right now."

Do you submit? No, because there is a higher law at that point. If your husband asks you to do something that is against God's law, you are not to submit. On the other hand, if what your husband is asking you to do doesn't violate any of God's commands, you submit to the best of your ability.

Peter's Perspective

"Wait a second," some wives are saying. "The Bible also says, 'Husbands, love your wives, just as Christ also loved the church.' If my husband isn't loving me as Christ loved the church, then I must not be obligated to submit to him. After all, if he is the initiator, if he is the one who should be taking the lead and is failing to do that, I'm not under any obligation to do my part."

First Peter chapter 3, however, contradicts this thinking:

Wives, likewise, be submissive to your own husbands, that even if some do not obey the word, they, without a word, may be won by the conduct of their wives, when they observe your chaste

*conduct accompanied by fear. Do not let your adornment be
merely outward—arranging the hair, wearing gold, or putting on
fine apparel—rather let it be the hidden person of the heart, with
the incorruptible beauty of a gentle and quiet spirit, which is very
precious in the sight of God. For in this manner, in former times,
the holy women who trusted in God also adorned themselves,
being submissive to their own husbands, as Sarah obeyed
Abraham, calling him lord, whose daughters you are if you do
good and are not afraid with any terror. (vv. 1–6)*

This passage deals with a Christian woman who is married to
a non-Christian man—and what she can do to reach her husband
for Christ. I also believe these verses apply to a Christian woman
who is married to a nominally Christian man, or a man who may
name the name of Christ, but has not stepped up into the role of
spiritual leader. God has given wives a positive strategy to follow in
reaching their husbands, and clearly lays out the role and responsibilities of the Christian wife in the marriage relationship.

In fact, as a wife begins to apply the principles found here, she
might even see her husband become a new-and-improved model.

The strategy for reaching your husband, Peter says, is "without a word." Here is a man who is an unbeliever, and his wife
wants him to come to faith. She might think, *Maybe I should just
hit him with a sermon every single day. I'll stuff Gospel tracts into
his shirt pockets. When he comes home from work, I'll preach to
him. I'll make him watch Christian TV programs with me.*

Though there is a place for declaring the Word, there is also
a place for *living* it. What you need to do is let God reach him by
the Holy Spirit, as you live out your radiant, Spirit-filled, Christ-
fragrant life.

What if you're married to an unbeliever? Sadly, this happens
all too often to single Christian women who get tired of waiting
on God and waiting for a Christian Mr. Right, and instead marry
some man who is not a follower of Jesus Christ.

Somehow they think the verse that says "do not be unequally
yoked together with unbelievers" (2 Corinthians 6:14) doesn't
apply to them. But then some time passes, and they are miserable in that relationship.

I have even had some of these women over the years come to me and say, "I've met this really great Christian man at church. God has told me that I can divorce my non-Christian husband and marry this Christian guy."

I've heard it the other way around, too. Christian guys have come to me and said, "God has told me that I can divorce my non-Christian wife and marry this great Christian woman."

My reply to that is: *No, He didn't.*

I can guarantee that God *did not* tell them this, because 1 Corinthians 7:13 says, "And a woman who has a husband who does not believe, if he is willing to live with her, let her not divorce him."

That sounds pretty clear to me. We also read in 1 Corinthians 7:27, "Are you bound to a wife? Do not seek to be loosed. Are you loosed from a wife? Do not seek a wife." So believers who are married to unbelievers should stick with that commitment and pray that the unbelieving spouse will come to his or her senses and come to the Lord.

How will that happen? More often than not it will come about because of how you live, more than what you say.

Live a godly life, and God will do the saving.

Inspiration or Manipulation?

Telling a woman that the way to reach her husband is by *not saying anything* is one of the most difficult things you could ask. Women, by nature, are very verbal, and gifted by the Creator with the ability to persuade. If this gift is yielded for good to God, it can have a profound influence. But if it is yielded for evil to Satan, it can be destructive.

For example, consider how Esther was able to use her feminine influence to rescue a whole generation of Jewish people. Then look at how Eve misused her feminine influence to move her husband in the wrong direction. Of course, Adam was responsible for what he did, but she helped facilitate the process.

You see, what wives must avoid is manipulation—trying to do

things that would move her husband to do what she wants him to do. Manipulation can be defined as "managing or influencing by artful or devious skill."

Wives must avoid this temptation to manipulate, because it will never bring about lasting change. I know it's tempting when he doesn't seem to be listening. You want to help out God a little bit, so you think, *I'll just weld the knob on his radio to a Christian station and then crank the volume all the way up... Or, I'll put little Gospel tracts in his sandwiches. Instead of turkey, it will be "The Four Spiritual Laws." Or, I'll get Christian guys to seek him out and try to talk to him.*

Most likely, he will see through all of that. He will know what you're trying to do, and may very well rebel from it. It will drive him away instead of drawing him in. Attempting to nag him into the Kingdom will not have the effect you were hoping for.

Solomon, who had many, many wives and knew a little bit about nagging, had this to say in Proverbs 19:13 (NLT): "A nagging wife annoys like a constant dripping." He also observed, "Better to dwell in the wilderness, than with a contentious and angry woman" (Proverbs 21:19).

Women nag when their husbands don't seem to be paying attention to them, so they keep pressing the point until hopefully he gets the message. But the fact of the matter is that nagging doesn't reach a man. Actually, it drives him away.

It's very easy to only pick up on the negatives in a marriage relationship. "You didn't take out the trash. Why don't you clean the toothpaste off the mirror? You didn't wash your whiskers down the sink. You left your tools out when you were working on the car. When are you going to fix this?"

Does all he hear about is what's *wrong* in your home and in your marriage? He also needs to hear about what's *right*. He needs to hear that you appreciate him…that you love him… that you find him attractive. Don't assume that men are so self-assured that they don't need to hear these things. They do. They need to be stroked a little bit. Maybe a lot. They need to be encouraged and reassured.

One reason a man often gets involved with another woman is because someone will come along and pay attention to him, and tell him he is so special and so wonderful. Then he goes home and perhaps never hears that from his wife. He even wonders at times if his wife still loves him. Wives need to verbally communicate their affection and appreciation to their husbands.

But the primary concept of the idea of winning your husband without a word is what could be described as "the silent preaching of a lovely life."[14] It is to first prepare the ground of his heart by living out your faith in the home. If you fail to do this, he will never listen to your message and will actually have an excuse for his unbelief. But on the other hand, if you break up the soil of his heart with your actions, your words will have far greater impact, and will eventually take root.

This same principle could be applied to other people in our lives who we want to win to Christ—be it parents, children, friends or coworkers. They don't need a sermon every day. They've heard your message. Now live it. Show yourself to be a Christian in practical, tangible ways, and that will open their hearts to the seed of the Word of God. They will see a distinct difference in your lifestyle as a result of your knowing Jesus Christ. That will speak volumes to them. A quote– often attributed to Saint Francis of Assisi– says, "Preach the Gospel, and when necessary, use words."[15]

Jesus told us that we are to be the salt of the earth and the light of the world (see Matthew 5:13–14). Many of us are light without being salt, and sometimes we are salt without being light. Being light without being salt means that we talk about our faith all the time—we proclaim it, but we aren't really living it.

Being salt means that we're having an effect on people around us, but maybe we're not talking about our faith as much as we should. There is a place for both salt and light. There is a place for testimony and speaking for Christ and a place for living the life. Both go hand in hand, and it's a powerful combination when it is empowered by God's Holy Spirit.

Looking Good

Returning to 1 Peter 3, we come to the subject of a Christian woman's outward appearance:

Do not let your adornment be merely outward—arranging the hair, wearing gold, or putting on fine apparel—rather let it be the hidden person of the heart, with the incorruptible beauty of a gentle and quiet spirit, which is very precious in the sight of God. For in this manner, in former times, the holy women who trusted in God also adorned themselves, being submissive to their own husbands. (vv. 3-5)

The word "adorning," used here, comes from the Greek word *cosmos*, from which we get the English word "cosmetic." Peter is talking about the emptiness of focusing on the outside while ignoring the inside.

As we look at this passage, it helps to understand the culture of the time. Roman women were given over to the latest fashion crazes, and were very focused on their looks. In fact, some of the engravings from this era indicate that women wore towering hairdos with nets of gold and expensive combs. They also wore gold rings and bracelets around their necks, ankles and arms. As a result, they would invest a great deal of time each day to their outward appearance.

Peter was essentially saying, "Bring this into balance. Don't flaunt your outward looks or make it your primary focus. Work on the attractiveness of your inner person as well." The phrase "putting on fine apparel" isn't saying that it's wrong for a Christian woman to be fashion-conscious or attractive.

Peter's point is simply this: Don't let clothing become your main focus in life. In fact, "putting on fine apparel" could be translated as "the frequent changing of clothing." It conveys the idea of a woman who is constantly changing her clothes for the purpose of impressing people. She wants everyone to notice how great she looks. Peter was saying, "Focus instead on the inner person. Think about the inside."

When it comes to this passage in Scripture, I'm sometimes asked, "What do you think about makeup? Should a woman wear makeup?" In answer to that, I quote Charles Swindoll: "Does [a house] need painting? Paint it!"[16]

Nevertheless, all of us, and especially women, need to be concerned with the *inside* of the house as well as the outside, because the inside is what really matters. This is what's really being addressed here.

In the description of the virtuous wife in Proverbs 31, we are told that she is aware of her outward appearance. She goes about her work with vigor and strengthens her arms. I don't know if she did arm curls or if they had Hebrew aerobics back then. But she is a woman who cares about the way she looks. In other words, a wife shouldn't go to the opposite extreme and neglect her appearance, either.

We hear the verse, "For bodily exercise profits a little" (1 Timothy 4:8), which is often quoted by overweight or out-of-shape people. While it's true that bodily exercise profits only "a little," at least it does profit *some*. The remainder of the verse says, "But godliness is profitable for all things, having promise of the life that now is and of that which is to come."

Think of it as temple maintenance. Your body is the temple of the Holy Spirit, and you should do what you can as a Christian woman to continue to be outwardly attractive to your husband. Even so, you should not do it at the expense of inward beauty.

Inner beauty is a very appealing quality that a Christian woman develops over the years. It is not achieved with makeup or clothes alone. Rather, it's a glow and a radiance that shines from the inside out.

What a marvelous quality this is in a godly woman. This is what 1 Peter 3:4 is speaking of: "Let it be the hidden person of the heart, with the incorruptible beauty of a gentle and quiet spirit, which is very precious in the sight of God." Or as another translation puts it, "The unfading loveliness of a calm and gentle spirit" (PHILLIPS).

Referring to "the hidden person of the heart," this phrase doesn't mean that a wife must sit around in silence and can't disagree with her husband or offer a different opinion. She certainly should speak her mind, and try to influence her husband for good. I would even venture to say that she has a God-given right and responsibility to set her husband straight if he's off-course.

I have come to highly value and respect my wife Cathe's opinions over the years. She has a way of seeing through a situation. I find that she often has discernment and observations about people that I might otherwise miss or overlook. She provides insight and wisdom, and that is virtue.

Love Him, but Like Him, Too

Finally, I want to point out that when the Scripture says that wives are to love their husbands, the word used for "love" in the original language is the Greek word *phileo*. As I mentioned in the previous chapter, this is one of several words for love in the Greek language.

It refers to a friendship love.

It is a given that wives should *agape* their husbands, which is a sacrificial, spiritual love. Yet wives are to *phileo* their husbands as well. Loosely translated, "Wives, *like* your husbands."

Don't just love him. Like him, and let him know.

Reassure him. He needs to hear that from you. And, let him lead—even if he doesn't do it perfectly. Let him make a few mistakes, but strengthen him in that leadership role, and don't undermine it by being overly critical or sarcastic. Don't try to make his leadership role difficult for him. Instead, make it easier. It's a lot of responsibility to bear, and it's not as easy as you might think.

Your husband needs your prayers, your support, and your encouragement. He needs to hear your commitment to him and your love for him reaffirmed.

So wives, submit to your husbands as to the Lord and win him without a word. Concentrate on the beauty of your inner person, even while maintaining an attractive outer appearance. How true it is when Scripture says, "Charm is deceitful and beauty is passing, but a woman who fears the LORD, she shall be praised" (Proverbs 31:30). Concentrate on the responsibilities God has given to you, and by the power of His Spirit, He will help you to be the woman He wants you to be.

If you are a husband reading this today and have, by God's grace, found yourself married to such a woman, don't take it for granted! Proverbs 18:22 says, "He who finds a wife finds a good thing, and obtains favor from the LORD."

If you have found a godly woman who is dedicated to Jesus Christ and has made a commitment to you, then you have a treasure of greater value than everything else on Earth.

Questions for Discussion

1. Before the Apostle Paul gives specific instructions regarding the critical roles of husbands and wives, he first gives the command, "Be filled with the Spirit." Why does this command have to come first?

2. Greg writes that God not only gives "refills" of the Holy Spirit throughout our day, but that we very much *need* such refills. What sorts of challenges and situations in marriage might benefit from a fresh filling of God's mighty Holy Spirit?

3. *"Be filled with the Holy Spirit…"* The Greek word translated as "fill" in this passage speaks of wind filling a sail. Greg writes: *"There is power, beauty and practicality in that picture of a wind-filled sail thrusting a boat forward through the waves."*

How might we use this word picture to describe a Spirit-filled, Spirit-directed, Spirit-empowered marriage relationship?

4. Another meaning for the Greek term "be filled" could be translated "to permeate," like salt permeating meat in order to preserve it. Greg writes: *"This tells us that the Holy Spirit wants to permeate our lives, touching everything we think, do, and say, entering every fiber of our being."*

What might this say about God's desire to touch and influence every aspect of married life—with none held back?

5. How does the verse "submitting to one another in the fear of God" (Ephesians 5:21) set the context for the specific instructions to wives and husbands that follows in verses 22-30?

6. Referring again to Ephesians 5:21, Greg writes: *"A husband's submission to his wife does not mean he abdicates his responsibility of leadership in the home. But it does mean that it helps her to bear her burdens."*

What does a husband's God-honoring submission to his wife look like in everyday life? Why is this sort of submission no danger to his responsibility of leadership?

7. Agree or disagree? *"A successful marriage…isn't so much about finding the right person as much as it is about BEING the right person."*

8. To those who struggle with the concept of the husband being the head of the home, Greg points them to Paul's words in 1 Corinthians 11:3. What do we learn from this passage? What does the submission of Jesus Christ to the Father tell us or illustrate for us about the submission of a wife to her husband?

9. Referring to the leadership of the husband in a marriage, Greg writes: *"Biblical leadership is servant leadership."*

What are some of the characteristics of a leader who is also a servant? Why is that kind of leadership easier to respond to?

10. Ephesians 5:22 reads: "Wives, submit to your own husbands, *as to the Lord."*

How might those last four words impact a wife's desire and motivation to follow this biblical imperative? Lay this scripture alongside Colossians 3:23. What parallels do you see between the two?

11. What is the responsibility of a wife whose husband asks her to submit to something immoral or illegal? How does the account in Acts 5:27-29 help us to gain perspective on this?

CHAPTER 6
Four Words That Can Change a Marriage

Therefore do not be unwise, but understand what the will of the Lord is.
–Ephesians 5:17

A man was walking along a Southern California beach and spotted an unusual-looking bronze object lying in the sand. He picked it up and began to dust it off, when all of a sudden, a genie appeared.

The genie told him, "Master, I will grant you one wish."

"One wish?" the man asked. "What happened to three wishes?"

The genie shrugged his shoulders and sighed. "You know how it is," he said. "With the economy and everything, we've had to cut back."

"Okay, I'll tell you what," the man said. "I love Hawaii, but I don't like to fly. If you could build me a highway from California to Hawaii so that I could drive there, that would be great. So that's my one wish. I want a highway from California to Hawaii."

"Give me a break!" the genie exclaimed. "There's no way I could do that. Think of the logistics involved! It's absolutely impossible. You'll need to choose something else."

The man thought about it for awhile. "Okay," he said quietly. "I think I have it now. I don't understand women at all—and especially my wife. My wish is that I would be able to understand women from this point forward."

The genie turned away for a moment, seemingly deep in thought. Then he turned back to the man and said, "Did you want that highway with two lanes or four?"

I wish I could share with you the magic key to understanding your wife, but having been married 38 years, I can honestly say I'm still a long ways away from that goal. Even though we husbands might have a hard time understanding our wives sometimes, we are still directed to love them (and really, they can be so lovable).

Every marriage, however, will face difficulties and challenges—even good marriages. In fact, sometimes this is what makes a good marriage. As we come through those difficulties, we learn how to bend, flex, and most importantly, how to love and forgive.

But we need to ask ourselves, "Am I as a husband doing my part in the marriage?" The question is not whether your wife is doing her part. *Put that question out of your mind.* The real issue is, are you doing yours? A failure to understand and apply the specific roles and responsibilities given to the husband and wife is the reason for the breakdown of so many marriages today.

Do you know what your responsibilities are? Scripture is actually quite clear on the subject. In fact, I'll venture to say that the bulk of the responsibility for the success of the marriage, in my opinion, rests squarely on the man's shoulders.

The truth is, many of us aren't being the leaders we ought to be. As a result, countless marriages are in trouble today because men are unwilling to obey God's specific commands.

So what are these commands? Let's look at some of them in Ephesians chapter 5.

Husbands, love your wives, just as Christ also loved the church and gave Himself for her, that He might sanctify and cleanse her with the washing of water by the word, that He might present her to Himself a glorious church, not having spot or wrinkle or any such thing, but that she should be holy and without blemish. So husbands ought to love their own wives as their own bodies; he who loves his wife loves himself. For no one ever hated his own flesh, but nourishes and cherishes it, just as the Lord does the church. For we are members of His body, of His flesh and of His bones. "For this reason a man shall leave his father and mother

*and be joined to his wife, and the two shall become one flesh." This
is a great mystery, but I speak concerning Christ and the church.
Nevertheless let each one of you in particular so love his own wife
as himself, and let the wife see that she respects her husband.*
(vv. 25-33)

Four Words

Here, then, are the four words that can change your marriage:

"Husbands, love your wives."

If husbands would "man up" and do what God calls them
to do, what a difference it would make—in the church, in our
world, in our culture.

Here's the problem: Even at our best, we men are prone to
fall into a pattern of passivity. And at our worst, we're dragging
everyone else down with us. There are far too many situations
where the man in the house is either indifferent to the things
of the Lord, or is an active hindrance to the rest of his family in
their search for God.

Passivity in a Christian man is tragic. This is a man who is simply
going through the motions in his walk with Christ, and has
lost the fire and desire he once had in past days.

"Oh sure, we can go to church," he might say. "But I'd really
rather watch the game on TV."

Come on, get up and be a man! *Lead* your wife. *Lead* your
children. Show them what a man of God looks like. This is the
gauntlet Paul throws down here in Ephesians 5.

Did you know that 90 percent of the books sold on the topic
of marriage and family are purchased by women?[17] The women
are out there buying the books, trying to find out how to follow
the Lord and be better wives. And the guys? Well, too many of
us are flipping through the channels, overly preoccupied with
work, or neck-deep in fishing, football or some other hobby.

The fact is, 70 to 80 percent of Christian books in general
are bought by women.[18] What's up with that? Don't men need to
learn? Don't men need to grow? Of course we do. And we need
to love our wives by leading the way in the Christian life.

A Second Look at "Love"

Someone might say, "Paul says to love my wife? What's so difficult about that?" First, you'd better understand a little about the Greek word Paul uses for "love" here.

In our English language, we basically have one word for "love." We use it to describe everything from "I love my dog" to "I love golf" to "I love my wife." Yet in Greek, the original language of the New Testament, there are several words for "love."

We discussed this in Chapter 5, but let's circle back and briefly examine those important terms again. There is eros, which primarily refers to love on the physical plane. This is where our English word "erotic" comes from. There is *phileo*, which is love on the emotional plane. The name "Philadelphia," meaning "house of brotherly love," derives from *phileo*. There is *storge*, which refers to family love, as in the love for parents or children.

Then there is *agape*, which speaks of a sacrificial, spiritual love.

This last word for love is a radical, self-giving, all-consuming love. It's the word used more often than any other in the Gospels to describe the love of God Himself. In John 3:16 we read, "For God so *agaped* the world, He gave His only begotten Son."

This is not to say that *eros*, and even *phileo*, don't have a part to play in a marriage. When you first saw your wife, you most likely found her physically attractive. So *eros* does play a part. Yet we tend to equate the word "erotic" with evil, because it's usually presented in a twisted and perverted manner. But *eros* is a God-given love, and in its proper place, has the blessing of the Lord. Of course, that proper place is within the parameters and safety of the marriage relationship...*and nowhere else*.

The sexual union between a husband and wife is a way to express their intimacy, their oneness with each other, and of course, for the purpose of bearing children. But it is something that God designed uniquely for a man and a woman who are committed in marriage to enjoy.

The problem with *eros* is that it's essentially selfish. *Eros* basically says, "I want something from you. Give it to me now."

While *eros* has its place, you can't build a marriage on it.

Then there's *phileo*. In many ways, *phileo* is a more noble love than *eros*, because *phileo* is a give-and-take love. It's really a love that says, "I love you if you love me," or "I love you as long as I find something lovable in you." *Phileo* is a love that expects something back—and springs from the sense of pleasure we draw from the object or the person loved. You feel good when you're with that person. He or she is fun to be with, makes you laugh, or entertains you. You love that person because of what he or she brings to the relationship, and you are loved for the same reason.

This world's love is primarily object-oriented. A person is loved because of their physical attractiveness, personality, wit, prestige, talent, or some other feature or trait we happen to find appealing. We love someone because they made it into *People* magazine's "50 Most Beautiful People" issue. Or we love the way they sing. We love the way they write. We love the way they do this or that. The problem is that this is a fickle kind of love. If the trait we find lovable—like beauty, for example—is diminished by age, or if someone more talented or gifted comes along, then this fickle love is transferred.

Here's the problem: Many people enter into marriage with nothing more than *eros* and *phileo*.

"I want this from you."

"I will love you as long as you are attractive to me, appealing to me, and I find what I want from you. But the moment you cease to do that for me, I'm moving on. I don't want you in my life anymore."

Then the marriage is dissolved because of so-called "irreconcilable differences."

In contrast to *eros* and *phileo*, *agape* springs from a sense of the preciousness of the object being loved. *Agape* is primarily determined by the character of the one who loves, and not necessarily whether the object is necessarily lovable. *Agape* is not a mere feeling or emotion. It is far more. This is the kind of love God commands us to have as husbands.

God commands us as husbands to love our wives with agape—

not with a fickle love dependent upon her day-to-day lovability. *Agape* loves in spite of all of that. This is a love that transforms the one being loved. As you love your wife like this, it will change her, just as Christ loved you like this and it changed you.

The husband who loves his wife for what she can give him loves as the world loves, and not as Christ loves. But the husband who loves his wife as Christ loves the church gives everything he has for his wife, including his own life, if necessary.

If a loving husband is willing to sacrifice his own life for his wife, then how much more should he be willing to make lesser sacrifices for her, such as his own likes and dislikes, desires, opinions, preferences and personal welfare? How much more should he be willing to set these aside to please her and meet her needs? He dies to self in order to live for his wife, because this is what Christ's love demands.

So instead of lecturing your wife on what she is supposed to do, why don't you look at what *you're* supposed to do? Make sure you are loving your wife as Christ loved the church.

A Man's Mission

Husbands, *agape* your wives.

Get after it. It's your mission, and God's clear command.

It's not just being "pleasant" or "nice" (though that's a good place to start). Rather, it is a deep affection and involvement, even if the object of that love seems unlovable at times.

"But Greg, she drives me crazy sometimes."

All right. So what?

"Well, it's really hard, because I don't find her attractive anymore. I did think she was attractive once, but she isn't anymore."

What does that have to do with it?

You need to love her as Christ loves the church, and you need to let her know that you love her.

I heard about a couple that was struggling, so they went to see a marriage counselor. After listening to the wife and the husband for a while, the counselor got up from his chair, came around to the front of his desk, and asked the wife to stand up. When she stood up, he put his arms around her and gave her a good hug. "This," he said to the husband, "is what your wife needs every single day from now on."

The husband replied, "What time do you want me to bring her back tomorrow?"

When was the last time you hugged your wife, without angling to get anything else? When is the last time you told her she's beautiful? It really doesn't do much good to *think* it, because she can't read your mind. You actually have to tell her, saying the words.

You say, "Well, the romance is gone in our marriage."

Then get it back.

Do what you did for her in the early days of your relationship. Set about winning her love and affection all over again. Don't wait for some random surge of emotion to get started—*just do it*, to borrow a popular phrase.

How about going on a date together? (And probably not to a cage fight or a demolition derby.) How about doing those simple things like opening a door for her, complimenting her or buying some little gift for her? Don't wait for the feeling of romance; *do romantic things*. If you do, the feelings will follow.

But even if the feelings don't follow, Scripture would tell you that for now you just have to tough it out and keep doing what God tells you to do. If you don't feel like it or if she doesn't respond—that doesn't matter! You have your marching orders from heaven itself.

Enter Her World

Another way to love your wife is to enter her world, to show some interest in the things that interest her.

"Frankly, Greg, my wife's interests bore me."

Then change your attitude, and get interested anyway. The Bible instructs men to dwell with their wives "according to knowledge."[19] That means *know* your wife. Know her likes and dislikes. Take time to understand her interests. The passage I quoted above goes on to say that if you don't live like this, your own prayers will be hindered. Did you know that? A man's prayer life can be crippled and rendered ineffective because he is out of alignment with his wife, and he has forgotten that she is supposed to be his best friend.

My wife is my best friend, and I'm not embarrassed to say that. She is my best friend, closest confidant and most valuable counselor. (She happens to be a very good cook, too.) Even so, Cathe and I are very different people. I don't naturally like a lot of the things that she likes.

For instance, my wife likes to watch cooking shows, often right before we go to sleep. Now this is a problem, because when I watch those shows I get hungry. She gets ideas, but I get hungry. When we go out to eat, she likes to order soup as an entrée. What? That's like a joke to me. Soup—or salad, for that matter—is *practice*. Soup is just a warm-up before the main event.

Yes, we're very different. But so what? I enter her world, as she enters mine. It's a partnership, walking this road together.

Let me ask husbands a question here. If you were walking down the street with your wife and kids, and a couple of rough-looking characters came toward you in a threatening manner, obviously intending to do harm to your family, what would you do? You'd defend them, of course. You'd deal with those thugs, and do whatever you had to do to shelter the lives of your wife and children.

Or what if your wife and your baby girl were starving, and had no food whatsoever. Would you try to find them some food somewhere?

"Well, of course," you say. "I'm a man."

Okay, but consider this. There are husbands today who have surrendered their roles of spiritual leadership. Their wives and children are being attacked by Satan and his minions while the men stand idly by and do nothing. Their families are starving spiritually, while these men won't lift a finger to help them and see them fed.

Yes, you would defend your wife physically and provide food and shelter for her. Well and good. *But how about doing it spiritually?* How about being a man of God and a leader in the home, and realizing that this is your calling.

"But Greg," you say, "she isn't submitting to me."

Well, she might…if you were doing *your* part. If we men would truly love our wives as Christ loves the church, they would respond more often as the church responds to Christ.

If you want your wife to blossom, to bloom, to be the woman of God that she can be, *start loving her like Jesus*. Value her. Treasure her. Honor her. Affirm her. Take time for her. And watch what happens. Again, stop worrying about *her* part—that will take care of itself. You concern yourself with your part.

The problem in many Christian marriages is that we're reading each other's mail, so to speak. The husband quotes verses that apply to his wife, and the wife counters with verses that apply to her husband. The truth is, we should be quoting verses to ourselves about what God has called each of us to do. If you take care of business and stay obedient to the Scriptures, you would be amazed at how your marriage could turn around.

Husbands Hold the Key

I keep repeating this, but that's okay. In fact, I'll probably repeat it a few more times before I'm done. I firmly believe that it is husbands who hold the key to a flourishing marriage, because they are the initiators. A wife will come into full fruition and submission in response to her husband loving her as he should.

If you think this sounds like a tall order, you're absolutely right. It is. But that is the example we are given to follow. How did Jesus Christ initially demonstrate His love toward us? It was through His death. In John 15:13, Jesus said, "'Greater love has no one than this, than to lay down one's life for his friends.'" Then in Romans 5:8 we read, "God demonstrates His own love toward us, in that while we were still sinners, Christ died for us."

We were once in rebellion against God, and our hearts were hardened against Him. But one day, we came into a realization of what Jesus did for us. Our hearts softened, and we responded and put our faith in Him. The Bible tells us, "We love Him because He first loved us" (1 John 4:19). So our love for Christ is a direct response of His persistent and patient love for us.

In the same way, a wife's respect of her husband and willingness to follow his leadership is rooted in his loving her as Christ loved the church. Just as the church has responded to Christ because of His overwhelming love, so will a wife respond to her husband for the same reason.

Our goal as husbands should be to simply fulfill God's command to us and leave her reaction up to Him. Why do we love her? So she will submit to us and follow us? No, we love her because we are commanded to.

It is our privilege, and our high calling.

The Leadership Paradox

So how do we do that? How do we lead and love like Jesus? Let's look at another passage:

> *Let nothing be done through selfish ambition or conceit, but in lowliness of mind let each esteem others better than himself. Let each of you look out not only for his own interests, but also for the interests of others.*

> *Let this mind be in you which was also in Christ Jesus, who, being in the form of God, did not consider it robbery to be equal with God, but made Himself of no reputation, taking the form of a bondservant, and coming in the likeness of men. And being found in appearance as a man, He humbled Himself and became obedient to the point of death, even the death of the cross. (Philippians 3:2-8)*

To love as Christ loves is to place my wife's needs ahead of my own. Remember, Jesus said, "For even the Son of Man did not come to be served, but to serve, and to give His life a ransom for many" (Mark 10:45). He came to serve. And following that example, husbands are to love and serve their wives.

Remember, before a word is given regarding the submission of a wife to her husband, the Bible tells us to submit to one another in the fear of God (Ephesians 5:21).

Returning to Philippians 2, we read in verse 7 that Jesus "made Himself of no reputation." Another way to translate this is, "He emptied Himself." Did He empty Himself of His divinity? Absolutely not. Never at any time did Jesus cease to be God. He never voided His deity, although you could say that He veiled it. What He did was to lay aside the privilege of deity when He walked among us as a man.

Although He was God, although He could do anything He wanted to, He allowed Himself to face the limitations of the human body. He experienced hunger, thirst, weariness and sorrow. He went through the range of human emotions. He emptied Himself of the privileges of deity, walked among us as a man, and He was our servant. This was so dramatically illustrated in the upper room when Jesus laid aside His outer garment, got down on His hands and knees, and washed the feet of the disciples. Truly, He humbled himself.

You may be thinking, *I'm not sure I could do that in my home. If I were to humble myself like that, my wife would walk all over me. She would take complete advantage of me.*

But that's not necessarily true.

And even if it were, so what?

Don't focus so much on her response. Just do what God has called you to do. Don't lecture your wife on what the Bible says to her; take heed to what the Bible says to you as a man and as a husband.

Here is something important to know about leadership: It is rooted in a paradox. The fact is, *true authority comes from humility.* It's not a matter of weakness, but of meekness. By meekness, I mean power under constraint. Your wife knows what you want to do; she knows what your desire is. But in loving her as Christ loves the church, you must be willing to surrender that.

So what does that mean in practical terms for us as husbands? Well, in my house, for starters, it means letting my wife have the remote control. This is very hard for me, because I'm the original channel-surfer. I'll start clicking that thing when a commercial comes on, because I hate commercials. From there, I'll surf along and watch about three minutes of a program, then go on to something else. I'll watch that for twelve seconds, then something else for ten minutes. Cathe will just start getting into a program, and then a commercial comes on. *Click*. I've moved on!

It drives her crazy. So for me to turn that remote control over to her is a pretty good expression of "dying to myself."

For you, dying to yourself and putting your wife's needs above your own might mean something else. I know it's hard to give up that control, but as I said, spiritual authority is rooted in paradox. Jesus said, "But whoever desires to become great among you shall be your servant. And whoever of you desires to be first shall be slave of all" (Mark 10:43–44).

In other words, true authority doesn't mean you manipulate your wife or lord it over her. That's not leadership—that's tyranny. In fact, a husband who constantly lectures his wife on his authority probably has very little.

This is not to say that a man shouldn't be firm and decisive and show leadership ability. But it does mean he is to be humble and unselfish. It means he is to rule with humility. It is what God asks of us: "He has shown you, O *man*, what is good; and what does the LORD require of you but to do justly, to love mercy, and to walk humbly with your God?" (Micah 6:8, *emphasis mine*).

Now I know this flies in the face of the stereotypical, macho-man concept of the tough guy who asserts himself, is always in control, and whose wife comes at his beck and call.

But that is not God's way.

Nor is it loving our wives as God has called us to. The fact is, it takes more courage, strength and discipline for a man to humble himself than to assert himself. What it takes is true love. And God requires nothing less.

Help or Hindrance?

Ephesians 5 goes on to say: "Husbands, love your wives, just as Christ also loved the church and gave Himself for her, that He might sanctify and cleanse her with the washing of water by the word" (vv. 25–26).

No one can be a greater hindrance to a wife's spiritual growth than her husband. But by the same token, no one can be a greater encouragement.

A husband's first priority is to make sure his wife is properly aligned with God. He recognizes that her personal happiness as a woman, a wife and a mother all hinge on that.

Some husbands might say, "That's her problem, not mine."

No, it is *your* problem.

Why? Because God has called us husbands to be the spiritual leaders in our homes, and to treat our wives with honor and care.

As we've already seen, the Apostle Peter tells us, "You husbands must be careful of your wives, being thoughtful of their needs and honoring them as the weaker sex. Remember that you and your wife are partners in receiving God's blessings, and if you don't treat her as you should, your prayers will not get ready answers" (1 Peter 3:7, TLB).

This is the same principle Jesus was speaking of when He said,

Therefore if you bring your gift to the altar, and there remember that your brother has something against you, leave your gift there before the altar, and go your way. First be reconciled to your brother, and then come and offer your gift. (Matthew 5:23–24)

We must take care of our home and lead. Our priorities should be: God first, then family, and then our occupations or ministries.

I know this is hard to do. It isn't any easier for me than it is for any other man. I have to consistently ask myself, am I loving my wife as Christ loves the church? Am I laying my life down? Am I being the leader God has called me to be? It's actually a constant process of realignment and fine-tuning, because we can be doing great as husbands and fathers one day, and fall short the next.

Ask for Help

You may be thinking, *You say I have to take the spiritual lead, and that the primary responsibility for my marriage and home rests on my shoulders. But that seems overwhelming to me! How can I do that? How can I pull it off? I can't.*

Quite honestly, *I can't either,* because these things don't come naturally for me. I'm not naturally wired to be humble, unselfish and focused on the needs of others. No one is.

So what do we do? In an earlier chapter we talked about the importance of being filled with the Spirit. We need Him so much! We absolutely can't accomplish these things on our own. We need supernatural help. This love that God commands for us to have for our wives has to come from Him, or it will never come at all.

I've been encouraged a number of times by the words of Romans 5:5, where Paul writes: "Now hope does not disappoint, because the love of God has been poured out in our hearts by the Holy Spirit who was given to us."

I don't have to squeeze *agape* love out of my heart like I'd squeeze juice out of an orange. Actually, I could squeeze forever and never get a drop. If I have God's love in my heart at all, it's because He is in the process of pouring it into me. And as He pours it in, I have the privilege of pouring it out. It will come as a result of walking closely with Him, because "the fruit of the Spirit is love" (Galatians 5:22).

You won't get there overnight. It will take a lifetime. But determine to move in that direction today and say, "I will be the man God has called me to be. From this day forward, I will seek to love my wife as Christ loved the church."

When the Attacks Come

Every marriage will come under attack. Every marriage, without exception, will weather some serious storms through the years.

It won't, however, be the severity of the storms that determine which marriages will survive, but rather the strength of their foundations.

As Jesus concluded a day of extraordinary teaching on a hillside, He told a story about two different men who each built homes.

Anyone who listens to my teaching and follows it is wise, like a person who builds a house on solid rock. Though the rain comes in torrents and the floodwaters rise and the winds beat against that house, it won't collapse because it is built on bedrock. But anyone who hears my teaching and doesn't obey it is foolish, like a person who builds a house on sand. When the rains and floods come and the winds beat against that house, it will collapse with a mighty crash. (Matthew 7:24-27, NLT)

We looked at this Scripture earlier, but as we consider it again, I want to ask this question: Is your marriage built on the rock…or are *you* on the rocks? If you have built on Christ the Rock and the timeless counsel of God's Word, your marriage will withstand those inevitable tests and storms of life.

Our marriage weathered the worst storm ever several years ago, when our 33-year-old son Christopher suddenly left for heaven after a car crash.

It broke my heart to see my wife trying to cope with this terrible, devastating event. Cathe loved Christopher, and had a very close relationship with him. It was difficult enough for me to deal with my own pain, but it was that much more agonizing to see my wife plunged into grief and mourning.

Through it all, however, I have seen qualities in Cathe's life that just blow my mind. I always knew she was a woman of God; she is Proverbs 31 right down the line. I wouldn't say that if I didn't mean it. She has been a tremendous example to me, through all the days of grief and healing.

Sometimes I wonder (if only for a minute), *What would it be like if we didn't have the Lord? What if we didn't have the hope of reunion in heaven? How could we have ever dealt with this? How could we have survived?* Even with the Lord, it's been very difficult. But through it all, our marriage has grown stronger than ever been before. Why? Because it is built on the Rock, and God has given us strength.

Yes, we try to live out these principles that God has given us in His Word. Do we do it perfectly? No, and I'm the first to admit that. But we're always working at it, applying ourselves—and really, that's a key right there.

We do work at it. We do cry out to God for His strength and wisdom.

And if you do the same, your marriage will stand…no matter what.

Questions for Discussion

1. *"Every marriage will face difficulties and challenges. … In fact, sometimes this is what makes a good marriage."*

Do you agree with this statement? In what ways can hardships or tough times actually strengthen a marriage? Why do crises bond some husbands and wives even closer together, while other marriages fall apart under such pressure? What makes the difference?

2. Isn't it natural for a husband to expect his wife to "do her part," as it's outlined in Scripture? Why then does Greg say that husbands need to banish that question from their minds?

3. Do you think Greg is overstating his case when he says that the ultimate responsibility for the success of a marriage rests directly on the man's shoulders? Why or why not?

4. Greg says one of the biggest problems men have—even Christian men—is falling into a pattern of passivity. Why does he assert that if men continue in that pattern, they will drag others down with them?

5. Greg writes about the tragedy of *"a man who is simply going through the motions in his walk with Christ, and has lost the fire and desire he once had in past days."* Since God truly expects a husband to be the spiritual leader in his home, how does his apathy and passivity effect everyone under his roof—and beyond?

6. "Husbands, love your wives" (Ephesians 5:25). Since *agape* is the Greek word for "love" in this verse *and* in John 3:16, what does that tell us about the nature, character and depth of that love?

7. *"If a loving husband is willing to sacrifice his own life for his wife, then how much more should he be willing to make lesser sacrifices for her—such as his own likes and dislikes, desires, opinions, preferences and personal welfare?"*

Is this statement a reasonable description of what the agape love of a husband for his wife ought to look like in a marriage, or does it go too far? What specific areas of daily life ought to be impacted by this determination?

8. In a further description of a husband's *agape* love for his wife, Greg states: *"It's not just being 'pleasant' or 'nice' (though that's a good place to start). It is rather a deep affection and involvement, even if the object of that love seems unlovable at times."*

What would a man's natural response be to a wife who has somehow become "unlovable"? What does this tell us about our huge need for supernatural ability to love as God calls us to love?

9. Greg states: *"Do what you did for her in the early days of your relationship. Set about winning her love and affection all over again. Don't wait for some random surge of emotion to get started—just do it."*

What kinds of behavior, conversation, planning and thoughtfulness characterize the "early days" of a romance? What could a husband do to begin winning the heart of his wife all over again? As Greg writes: *"Don't wait for the feeling of romance; do romantic things. If you do, the feelings will follow."*

10. Husbands, how can you begin to enter your wife's world (even a little bit) as you practice the selfless *agape* love that is sourced in God?

11. Read again the Lord's analogy in Matthew 7:24-27. What can you and your spouse do to prepare your marriage for the inevitable storms and floods that—sooner or later—batter every home?

CHAPTER 7
What Jesus Taught About Marriage & Divorce

"Moses provided for divorce as a concession to your hardheartedness, but it is not part of God's original plan. I'm holding you to the original plan, and holding you liable for adultery if you divorce your faithful wife and then marry someone else." –Matthew 19:8-9, THE MESSAGE

Our contemporary culture has plenty to say about marriage—and much of it is mocking, cynical, negative, or downright hostile. In the 1950s and '60s, television programs like *Leave It to Beaver, Ozzie and Harriet, Father Knows Best* and a host of other nightly offerings held up secure, traditional marriages and happy families as models to emulate.

No longer.

For years now, faithful husbands and wives, dedicated dads, devoted mothers, and secure, happy kids have been minimized, discounted, parodied and ridiculed. Movies glorify the "adventure" of adulterous relationships, and portray men and women who choose to remain virgins until marriage as strange, eccentric people who are only to be pitied.

Yes, we certainly get an eyeful and earful from the world around us about marriage and divorce. But what does the Bible have to say? What is the biblical worldview?

I hope you're not looking to celebrity culture for your cues on how to have a successful marriage.

Standing in line to check out at your local grocery store will keep you up to date (whether you want to be or not) on all the latest hookups, breakups, heartbreaks and betrayals. As the covers of multiple gossip magazines attest, these Hollywood luminaries can't even seem to keep a relationship together, much less a marriage. The partner-swapping happens so rapidly you can't keep track of it all without a program.

No, you won't get much information on building a successful marriage from the tabloids. The Bible, though, has a great deal to say on the subject, and its information is as relevant today as it was two thousand years ago.

Jesus Challenges the Assumptions

In His Sermon on the Mount, Jesus had been challenging some old and deeply held assumptions—to the amazement of His listeners. Beginning with the phrase "you have heard that it was said" (NIV), He took on one traditional opinion and long-held conviction after another, contrasting those teachings with God's actual intent and heart desire.

By the time He came to the subject of marriage, divorce and adultery, He must had everyone's almost breathless attention.

It has been said, 'Whoever divorces his wife, let him give her a certificate of divorce.' But I say to you that whoever divorces his wife for any reason except sexual immorality causes her to commit adultery; and whoever marries a woman who is divorced commits adultery. (Matthew 5:31-32)

Some time later, He had occasion to add to those remarks:

The Pharisees also came to Him, testing Him, and saying to Him, "Is it lawful for a man to divorce his wife for just any reason?"

And He answered and said to them,

"Have you not read that He who made them at the beginning 'made them male and female,' and said, 'For this reason a man shall leave his father and mother and be joined to his wife, and the two shall become one flesh'? So then, they are no longer two but one flesh. Therefore what God has joined together, let not man separate." (Matthew 19:3-6)

It's interesting how Jesus immediately answers the Pharisees' question by flashing back to the beginning of time, and the creation of Adam and Eve. And why not? He was there! No one could know better how God had intended the husband-wife relationship to work than the One who invented it in the first place.

Adam, of course, had the ultimate setup, as we noted in Chapter 2. Talk about the best bachelor pad ever! He had all the delicious food he wanted to eat, meaningful work and responsibility, the whole wild and entertaining animal kingdom for companionship, and of course the daily fellowship of the Lord Himself.

As time went by, however, and Adam noted the males and females of all the species and how they always walked together, sharing their food, their nests and dens, and brought up their little families, he must have felt something missing.

An ache? An empty place? Or was it just an inner, deep-down knowledge that his life wasn't complete?

So as we have seen, God created the perfect companion, friend and lover in the lovely person of Eve. Reflecting on that moment, commentator Matthew Henry wrote:

> *Eve was made by God not out of [Adam's] head to rule over him, nor out of his feet to be trampled upon by him, but out of his side, to be equal with him. Under his arm to be protected, and near his heart to be loved.* [20]

When you think about it, Adam and Eve had everything you would want for an ideal marriage. She would never have to hear about the way his mother cooked, and he didn't have to hear about all of the other men she could have married!

So that's the way Jesus chose to open the subject. Before He spoke to the tragedy of divorce, He first walked the Pharisees back to a beautiful Garden at the beginning of time, and a man and woman lived together and loved one another without so much as a shadow of conflict.

The Seismic Destruction of Divorce

I would venture to say that everyone reading these words has been impacted in some way by divorce. Perhaps you have experienced that heartache personally. Then again, it may be that your parents or your children or a close friend has been divorced. You've seen it up close, and in some way, shape or form, it has cast its long shadow across your life.

Certainly, divorce is on the rise in our culture. According to statistics, there now is one divorce for every 1.8 marriages.[21] Over a million children a year are involved in divorce, and without question, it is wrecking havoc on our country. As Pope John Paul II well said, "As the family goes, so goes the nation."[22]

Through the years I have noted that most of our nation's ills can be directly traced to the breakdown of the family. If ever there was a time we needed to do everything we can to keep our marriages together, the time is now.

It seems people will dissolve their marriages over practically anything these days. People say to themselves, *This is just too hard. I'll end this marriage and slide into a new relationship. It will be a new beginning for me, and I'll leave all my problems and heartaches behind*. What people discover, however, is that their problems follow right behind them into the new relationship, and they're every bit as unhappy as before—or even more so.

When it comes to marriage and divorce, there is no such thing as a "clean break." Divorce is very, very messy, and it always will be.

In the book *Second Chances*, psychologist and researcher Judith Wallerstein wrote:

> *Divorce can be deceptive. Legally it's a single event, but psychologically it's a chain. Sometimes a never-ending chain of events, relocations and radically shifting relationships strung through time, a process that forever changes the lives of the people involved.*[23]

When is divorce permissible for believers? Ever?

Yes, there are biblical grounds for divorce, but the number-one reason couples cite for ending their marriage is "irreconcilable differences."

That phrase drives me crazy. Irreconcilable differences? Everybody has irreconcilable differences. My wife and I have had them for nearly 40 years. She's very neat; I'm often messy. She tends to be late; I'm usually early. She likes the toilet seat down; I like it up. (I'm still working on that one. Even my little granddaughter scolds me. "Papa, put the toilet seat down!")

It's a funny thing. Some of the very qualities that attracted you to your mate in the beginning somehow morph into issues that divide you. Why did you like this person in the first place? Because he or she was different than you! She was outgoing and talkative; you were more quiet and reserved. He was creative and impulsive; you were practical and cautious.

And now it's driving you crazy? Now it's an "irreconcilable difference"? Give me a break! Why can't these differences—*any* differences—be resolved in the strength and grace of Jesus Christ? Sometimes you just have to take a deep breath, square your shoulders, and say, "This thing may never change, but I made a vow to stand by my mate for richer or poorer, for better or for worse, in sickness and in health. I'm going to love him anyway. I'm going to stick with her through it all."

The Bible doesn't recognize "irreconcilable differences" as a reason to dissolve a marriage.

In Jesus' day, there was a very lax attitude toward marriage. The divorce laws were heavily weighted in favor of men, and a man could divorce his wife for pretty much any reason. According to one liberal rabbi of the day, you could send your wife away for "incompatibility of temperament." (Which sounds a lot like "irreconcilable differences" to me.) A man could also divorce his wife for such trivial things as burning his meal, embarrassing him in front of his friends, or letting her hair down in public. And according to the rabbi known as Akiba, a man could send his wife away simply because another, more attractive woman came along.[24]

How absurd. Yet this was the prevalent attitude in the day when the Pharisees posed their question to Christ.

Looking a little more closely at the text of Matthew 19, I'd like to note carefully a couple of words. In verse 7 (NIV), the Pharisees said, "Why then did Moses command that a man give his wife a certificate of divorce and send her away?"

Jesus answered them, but changed a key term. He said, "Moses permitted you to divorce your wives because your hearts were hard" (v. 8).

They said *commanded*. Jesus said *permitted*. Moses didn't "command" any man to divorce his wife. But because of the hardness and callousness of a man's heart, Moses permitted what amounts to a release clause for the sake of the woman. This provision in the law allowed her to escape from the hardship of trying to carry on in a home where she was unloved and unwanted, because a man had failed to live up to the high ideal of marriage.

So When Is Divorce Allowed?

#1: Divorce is allowed when sexual immorality takes place.

Again, it is not commanded. But it is allowed. Matthew 19:9 says, "I say anyone who divorces his wife, except for sexual immorality, and marries another, commits adultery."

Back in our Sermon on the Mount text, Jesus said in Matthew 5:32, "Whoever divorces his wife for any reason except sexual immorality commits adultery."

Okay…but what is sexual immorality? The biblical term comes from the Greek *pornea*. (We get the word "pornography" from this word.) It speaks of extramarital sexual relations, including the so-called "affair." This includes any sex outside of marriage, including incest, prostitution and homosexuality.

Why is immorality a potential deal-breaker in a marriage? Because the oneness of the marriage bond has been violated. Paul even said, "Do you not know that he who unites himself with a prostitute is one with her in body?" (1 Corinthians 6:16, NIV)

Yes, you could call it a "one-night stand" or a "fling."

You could say it didn't really mean anything.

But it means a lot to God, and it should mean a lot to you. When you have sex with someone besides your spouse, you enter into a union with that person, and violate the union between you and your mate.

Having said all that, however, you don't have to get a divorce if immorality has taken place. In fact, I would even say that every effort should be made to restore the marriage. Both partners should examine the steps that led to this sin, and apply some preventative measures.

But by all means, try to save the marriage.

Immorality is not only grounds for divorce, *it is also grounds for forgiveness*.

#2: Divorce is allowed when desertion takes place.

In 1 Corinthians 7:13 (NIV), Paul says that "if a woman has a husband who is not a believer and he is willing to live with her, she must not divorce him."

So we have a Christian who has been united in marriage to a non-Christian. How does this happen? It happens because of disobedience. It happens in spite of the Bible's clear warning against an "equal yoke" in marriage (2 Corinthians 6:14).

A Christian will become impatient waiting to find that right guy or that right girl, and marry the first person who becomes available. Then, as time goes by, the believer invariably realizes he or she should never have done that, and sometimes they start looking for the back door.

Again, here is what Scripture tells us: "If a woman has a husband who is not a believer and he is willing to live with her, she must not divorce him."

Your job description now, Christian woman, is to win that man to Christ. The passage goes on to say: "For perhaps the husband who isn't a Christian may become a Christian with the help of his Christian wife. And the wife who isn't a Christian may become a Christian with the help of her Christian husband. Otherwise, if the family separates, the children might never come to know the Lord; whereas a united family may, in God's plan, result in the children's salvation" (1 Corinthians 7:14, TLB).

But let's say the nonbeliever departs—he or she abandons you. Paul goes on to say in 1 Corinthians 7 that in such cases, a brother or a sister is not "under bondage," because God has called us to peace.

The phrase used there for "under bondage" means held by consent of agreement, or to be a slave of. So if the nonbeliever leaves, you are free.

But what if he or she claims to be a Christian? It doesn't matter. It's the leaving that matters, not whether the departing partner claims to know Jesus. Quite frankly, if any man or woman would leave their spouse—claiming the leading of the Lord—when that spouse wants them to stay, I would have to question if that person was a Christian at all. The Bible says, "If anyone does not provide for his relatives, and especially for his immediate family, he has denied the faith and is worse than an unbeliever" (1 Timothy 5:8, NIV).

The proof of our faith is not just in what we say; it is in what we *do*.

So if your spouse abandons you, if he or she leaves you, according to Scripture you are not held to the agreement any longer.

Divorce Ought to Be Very Rare

Again, however, try to keep your marriage together at all costs. Most of us really have no idea of the utter devastation that divorce brings. In a book titled *The Divorce Revolution*, the author made this statement:

> *Divorce and separated people have the highest admission rates to psychiatric facilities. It takes its toll on the physical well-being of the people. Divorced people have more illness, higher mortality rates, and higher suicide rates.*[25]

And that's not even to mention the children.

Some time ago, a *Newsweek* article noted:

> *The emotional wounds [of the children of divorce] run deep–and time does not always heal. Divorce remains a central issue throughout their lives no matter how well adjusted they may seem. A hole in the heart is uNIVersal. ...There is a sense of having missed out on something that is a birthright, the right to grow up in a house with two parents.*

> *Compared with people who have grown up with intact families, adult children of divorce are more likely to have troubled relationships, broken marriages. A desire for stability sends some down the aisle at too young an age and they end up in divorce court not long afterward.*[26]

So much for that despicable old fiction about children of divorce being "resilient."

Here's the bottom line: Divorces that have a legitimate basis in Scripture are extremely rare. Trust me on this one. Through all my years of ministry, *most* divorces I have seen could have been avoided if the husband and wife would have humbled themselves and simply began obeying the Word of God.

That's where it all begins, of course—with a commitment to obey God. It continues with an ongoing commitment to daily (and even hourly) trust God, drawing on His life, wisdom, joy and power, even when times are very, *very* tough.

Can we say that we will submit ourselves and our marriage to what the Word of God says? Can we commit to trying to do this God's way, instead of the world's way?

With God's help, periodically take stock of your marriage and see if there's anything that might be bringing division between you and your spouse. If you identify it, whatever it is, get rid of it.

Your goal is to leave and cleave.

Yes, the storms will come. Great dark storms you can track as they roll over the horizon, and sudden, unexpected storms that rip through your life like a flash flood under a clear blue sky. The temptations and attacks will come, too. The bottom line? You'd better do what you can now to protect your marriage and your home from the perils that will surely come.

A few years ago Southern California faced terrible firestorms fanned by the relentless Santa Ana winds. I remember reading about one man's home in a wooded area that had somehow survived a fire that destroyed the homes in his neighborhood.

The newspaper showed a huge photo of a blackened, devastated area, with this man's home—gleaming, white and seemingly untouched—in the midst of it.

They asked this man, "What's your secret?"

"I just went above code for building," he replied. "I sealed the eaves. I used double-paned glass. I went above and beyond the requirements of everything they said." So when the fire came, it didn't burn his house.

In the same way, we need to do what we can to defend our homes against the fires of hell that would like to burn them to the ground.

It takes some extra caution and extra preparation. It means going the extra mile, and refusing to "just get by" with the bare minimum. It means giving it your all, and really working at this practice of leaving and cleaving. It means determining in your heart that your wife or your husband will be your best friend and confidant.

As you do your part to shore up your home, it will still be standing when the flames roar overhead and torch other homes and marriages all around you.

And the effort will be worth it. A million times over.

Questions for Discussion

1. Why did Jesus answer the Pharisees' specific question about divorce by taking them back to the Garden of Eden?

2. Greg writes: *"Through the years I have noted that most of our nation's ills can be directly traced to the breakdown of the family. If ever there was a time we needed to do everything we can to keep our marriages together, the time is now."*

If our nation's ills can indeed be traced back to the systematic destruction of our marriages and families, what positive impact can even one intact, happy, God-centered marriage have on an apartment complex…a block…a neighborhood…or a city?

3. Sometimes people contemplating divorce imagine that ending their marriage will be a quick escape or fresh new beginning to life. What factors are they failing to take into consideration?

4. Greg challenges the notion of so-called "irreconcilable differences" and cites how very different he is from his wife in so many ways. The fact is, any difference can be reconciled in the strength and grace of Jesus Christ. Describe the mindset and commitment necessary in a marriage to face up to differences and "work things out" with the help of Almighty God.

5. Greg reflects: *"It's a funny thing. Some of the very qualities that attracted you to your mate in the beginning somehow morph into issues that divide you. Why did you like this person in the first place? Because he or she was different than you!"*

Think of the differences between you and your spouse that once attracted you, and now annoy you. What has changed? Have those differences become more pronounced, or have you become less patient and more self-centered?

6. Why is immorality a potential deal-breaker in a marriage? And do such sins mean that divorce is inevitable? What are some possible advantages of working through the pain, anger and heartbreak of marital infidelity in order to preserve a marriage?

7. According to 1 Corinthians 7:13-14, what is the opportunity and "job description" of a Christian spouse who is married to a non-Christian husband or wife?

8. Greg tells the story of a man who lived in a densely wooded neighborhood who went the extra mile to protect his home in the event of a forest fire. He succeeded by going beyond the suggested building codes and taking more precautions than anyone required or expected. As a result, his home was left standing when the rest of the neighborhood went up in flames. How can you bring that same sort of above-and-beyond care, preparation and precaution to your marriage, the most valuable human relationship of your life?

CHAPTER 8

Caught in the Act

"All right, hurl the stones at her until she dies. But only he who never sinned may throw the first!" –John 8:7, TLB

A recent newspaper article described the plight of two thieves who had broken into a home and stolen electronic equipment.

After they were safely away with their haul, one thief asked his partner, "Did you notice there was a parrot back in that house?"

The other burglar had noticed, and said, "Yeah, I saw that. Do you think he heard me refer to you by name? And what if he heard the name and is now repeating it?"

So, fearing the parrot might turn into a stool pigeon, they decided they had to go back and steal the bird, too. As they were removing the parrot (whose name was Marshmallow) from the premises, however, someone called the police, and the thieves were arrested.

Aren't you glad thieves are stupid? They were caught in the act, because they'd been afraid "a little bird would tell their story."

I read another story about a thief who decided to steal some sausages from a meat market. (This is also a true story.) He grabbed one and began running, not realizing that it was part of a string of sausages 45 feet long. He tripped and fell making his getaway, became tangled in the sausages, and when the police officers found him, he was completely immobilized.

Caught in the act!

In yet another "true crime" story, I read about a 14-year-old who attempted to steal gas from a man's RV in Seattle. Sticking a short hose into the motor home's tank, he sucked hard to get the gas flowing. Dennis Quigley, the owner of the RV, heard noises outside, went out to investigate—and found the teenager collapsed in a heap, vomiting violently. Unfortunately for the young thief, he had put the hose into the sewage tank instead of the gas tank.

Quigley decided not to bring charges against the boy. He told the police he thought the young thief "had suffered enough."

Caught in the act!

Have you ever been caught in the act of doing something you shouldn't have been? In John 8, we have the account of a woman who experienced the shame and terror of being caught in the very act of adultery.

According to the law of the day, she could have been put to death by stoning. That sentence, however, was never carried out, and she never received the punishment the law required. In her sin, humiliation and dread, she had been brought to the feet of Jesus, and what could have been the worst day of her life became the very best day of her life.

Springing the Trap

Jesus returned to the Mount of Olives, but early the next morning he was back again at the Temple. A crowd soon gathered, and he sat down and taught them. As he was speaking, the teachers of religious law and Pharisees brought a woman they had caught in the act of adultery. They put her in front of the crowd.

"Teacher," they said to Jesus, "this woman was caught in the very act of adultery. The law of Moses says to stone her. What do you say?"

They were trying to trap him into saying something they could use against him, but Jesus stooped down and wrote in the dust with his finger. They kept demanding an answer, so he stood up again and said, "All right, stone her. But let those who have never sinned throw the first stones!" Then he stooped down again and wrote in the dust.

When the accusers heard this, they slipped away one by one, beginning with the oldest, until only Jesus was left in the middle of the crowd with the woman. Then Jesus stood up again and said to her, "Where are your accusers? Didn't even one of them condemn you?"

"No, Lord," she said.

And Jesus said, "Neither do I. Go and sin no more."

Jesus said to the people, "I am the light of the world. If you follow me, you won't be stumbling through the darkness, because you will have the light that leads to life." (John 8:1-12, NLT)

The Pharisees, no doubt, had stayed up all night hatching their scheme—setting up a foolproof trap they intended to spring on the Teacher from Galilee. Their desire was to have Him arrested. But in order for that to happen, they had to find some charge to bring against Him.

It's easy to imagine the Pharisees and experts in the law huddling together to think of some way, some pretext, that would allow them to arrest Jesus—and silence His voice once for all.

Someone finally came up with an idea. "I've got it," he would have said. "We'll get a woman caught in the act of adultery, bring her into His presence, and say, 'What should be done to her?' Everyone knows that the Law says to stone her. If He says, 'Yes, do what the law says,' then the people will withdraw from His just but distant touch. But then again, if He says, 'Don't stone her,' we'll accuse Him of breaking the Mosaic Law. Either way, He's going to fall into our trap. This is foolproof."

The first order of business, however, was to entice a woman into their snare, and then set her up to be caught and condemned.

Even though it was a total setup, this doesn't excuse the woman's actions. She was clearly guilty of immorality, and Jesus never disputed that fact. It's even possible that one of the very men who brought this woman before Jesus was the individual involved in the act of adultery with her. Notice that they didn't bring the offending man before the Lord, just the woman. In the Mosaic Law, you were supposed to bring both parties forward.

Nevertheless, it all went according to plan. They caught this woman in a compromising position, and dragged her to the temple courtyard, where they knew they would find Jesus teaching.

After that, nothing went according to plan.

Eleven verses later, Jesus had turned the tables on them, and they walked away humiliated…while the woman went free. The issue had suddenly become *their* sin, rather than the sin of the woman they had tricked and betrayed.

This incident reminds us that just because someone quotes Scripture doesn't mean they are necessarily walking closely with God. In fact, those who are the quickest to quote Scripture in order to condemn others are frequently the guiltiest of all. I've seen it time and again: The biggest faultfinders and nitpickers are often guilty of worse sin in their own lives. How wise Jesus was in His Sermon on the Mount to tell us all:

> *Why do you look at the speck of sawdust in your brother's eye and pay no attention to the plank in your own eye? How can you say to your brother, 'Let me take the speck out of your eye,' when all the time there is a plank in your own eye? You hypocrite, first take the plank out of your own eye, and then you will see clearly to remove the speck from your brother's eye. (Matthew 5:3-5, NIV)*

In other words, you're so quick to point out a minor fault in someone else, when you are guilty of something far worse. And that is certainly the case in the story before us. The accusers themselves were guilty of gross sin, and didn't care one bit about this woman or her dilemma. They wouldn't have blinked an eye if she had been stoned to death on the spot. How hard their hearts had become!

"Overtaken in Any Trespass…"

> *Brethren, if a man is overtaken in any trespass, you who are spiritual restore such a one in a spirit of gentleness, considering yourself lest you also be tempted. Bear one another's burdens, and so fulfill the law of Christ. (Galatians 6:1-2)*

What should we do if we know of a fellow believer who has compromised his or her standards and fallen into the sin of adultery?

The Scripture above doesn't say "condemn that person and make sure you tell as many people as you can."

Notice that the objective in Galatians 6:1-2 is to restore, not to condemn or destroy.

Yes, a fellow believer who is involved in adultery needs to be confronted and told that what they are doing is wrong. But if they are willing to turn from their sin, we need to do everything we can to lift them back up.

Why? Because the Scripture says, *"considering yourself lest you also be tempted."* Why should you help a person who has fallen into sin? Because one day it might be you who needs help. One day you might stumble and fall, and you will find yourself hoping and longing for someone to treat you with gentleness and respect, help you back on the right pathway, and redirect your ways toward God.

Besides that, our adversary the devil would love push us into the very same snare that we've sought to help a brother or sister escape from.

Hebrews 2:1 says, "Therefore we must give the more earnest heed to the things we have heard, lest we drift away."

Sadly, there are many people, even in the church, who are falling into this sin today. At this very moment, all of us could readily bring to mind the faces of friends, acquaintances or family members who have fallen into fornication or adultery.

Maybe it's a temptation you're struggling with yourself, even as you read this chapter.

I heard about a young preacher who was preaching on this heavy subject, and thought he would lighten things up a bit. He had heard a well-known evangelist use a joke about adultery. The evangelist had said to the crowd, "I have spent some of the happiest moments of my life in the arms of another man's wife." Pausing for dramatic effect, he added, "…and that woman was my mother."

The young pastor liked that joke, and made a mental note to use it on the right occasion. The moment seemed to arrive during his sermon on adultery. With a little smile, he announced to the congregation, "I have spent some of the happiest days of my life in the arms of another man's wife."

And then suddenly his mind went blank. He couldn't remember the punch line!

After a long (and very awkward) pause he said, "…and for the life of me, I can't remember who she was."

So the joke backfired, and believe me, I know the feeling. I've had plenty of jokes backfire on me in the pulpit.

Obviously, adultery is no laughing matter. How many lives have been destroyed by it? How many homes and families have been blasted apart, right down to the foundations, by this devastating sin? And of course it isn't just the actual act of adultery that is a sin, but all the things that go with it. Adultery is always accompanied by a pattern of hypocrisy, deception, lying and attempts to cover up the guilt.

I read an article not long ago in *USA Today* with the headline: "Business Scandals Prompt Look Into Personal Lives." The article pointed out that those who had committed corporate fraud were, in most cases, also guilty of infidelity.

I found one comment in the article especially interesting:

> *If their life is a lie, it is not confined to their personal life. If they are lying to their wives, there is also huge potential they are lying to their colleagues, to the board of directors and to their auditors.*[27]

It's true. Lies and deception in one area of life tend to leach, like toxic sludge, into every other area of life. In other words, very soon you won't just be living a lie, you will be a lie.

"Don't Do This…"

I received a letter some time ago from a man who had attended our church for awhile. He'd had a ministry along with his wife, and then fell into the sin of adultery. Later, after the destruction was done, he wrote to me and told me what happened. Here is what he said, in his own words:

> *Dear Greg,*
>
> *As you may know, Mary and I are no longer husband and wife. Our marriage ended in divorce. Bottom line Greg, I took my eyes off God and placed them on circumstances surrounding me. Pride, lust and the enemy had their way. Before long Mary, God's gift to*

*me, no longer satisfied me and I committed adultery. In fact, the
very night that act took place you and I crossed paths at the mall.*

I remembered that particular occasion well. I had been strolling through this mall, and he was in one of those little food-court restaurants out in the open. I noticed that he was sitting at a table with a woman who was not his wife.

This is strange, I'd thought. *What should I do?*

My first inclination was to just walk on by and not say anything. But then I thought, *Who knows what he's up to. Maybe I ought to just go up there and see what's going on.* So I decided to walk right up to him and his female companion.

"Hey, John," I said, "how are you doing?"

He appeared very uneasy and uncomfortable. "Oh, hi, Greg." I stood there for a few minutes talking to him, making sure to ask about his wife.

"How's Mary doing?"

"Oh, she's fine. Everything's going well."

He never introduced the girl to me, so I asked him, "Well, who is this here?"

"This is Christy, and I work with her."

I walked away, fervently hoping nothing was going on. I wanted so much to believe that it was all innocent, but somehow the situation didn't ring true. Here's what John went on to say in his letter to me:

*I was there in the restaurant with a co-worker I introduced
as Christy. Remember? When I look back on that night, I am
reminded of when Judas came to Jesus in the garden with a band
of soldiers to arrest Jesus. And before Judas identified Christ to the
mob with a kiss, Jesus said to him, "Friend, why have you come?"
In that moment Jesus was giving to Judas one more opportunity
to turn to Him. Greg, you were that person God used to cross my
path that evening to wake me up, to warn me, don't do this.*

*I didn't listen. Needless to say that decision and those that
followed would systematically destroy my life. I hit rock
bottom. My life was in complete shambles. I lost everything. My
relationship with God. My marriage. My reputation. Everything
was gone. I look back on my life now and see the destruction
that has been done through my selfishness. I failed to take God*

seriously at His Word, because I thought, "I know what I'm doing. Get out of my way, God, you're crowding me."

As a result, I virtually destroyed what life I had at the time. Even worse, I destroyed Mary's life as well. Not to mention all those folks whose lives we had impacted for God.

What a sad story. Yes, God forgave John, and Mary remarried, and has found happiness in her new marriage. But it didn't have to be. What a tragedy took place here because John chose to disobey God.

Why do I tell this story? Simply to underline my point: Adultery is pure poison. Adultery wounds, scars, withers, kills and tears into the fabric of a marriage and a home like nothing else. Our 21st-century culture—with its books, magazines, movies and celebrities—seems to work overtime to make adultery seem trivial, natural, no-big-deal, and even to be expected.

But it's all a lie. It's like whitewashing a tomb full of rotting bones.

The book of Proverbs says, "Adultery is a brainless act, soul-destroying, self-destructive" (6:32, THE MESSAGE).

What the world calls an "affair" or an "indiscretion" is in reality a sin that will wound you and others to the very core, and will affect you for the rest of your life.

Six Reasons Not to Commit Adultery

It seems crazy to even list reasons against committing adultery. Aren't they obvious? Nevertheless, I do it remembering the Scripture we quoted earlier: *"...considering yourself lest you also be tempted."* In other words, none of us is immune. No matter who we are, we are never beyond the reach of devastating, life-shattering sin. The moment you allow yourself to think, *It could never happen to me*, watch out!

That is why I list the following reasons below. Why should I avoid the sin of adultery?

#1. Adultery does incredible damage to your spouse.

In 1 Corinthians 6:18 (NIV), the Apostle Paul writes: "He who unites with a prostitute is one with her in body." When you committed your life to your wife or husband, the two of you became one flesh. But if you have sex with someone else, you violate that oneness with your spouse and enter into a oneness with that other person.

A one-night stand?

Don't deceive yourself. There is no such thing.

This is why Jesus gave a release clause from the marriage because of the seriousness of this offense. That is *not* to say that if you have been unfaithful to your spouse that they should divorce you, or vice versa. As I noted in the previous chapter, adultery is not only grounds for divorce, it is also ground for forgiveness. I encourage you to forgive your spouse and give them another chance.

#2: Adultery does incredible damage to yourself.

To even get to this place where you're willing to commit adultery means that you've had to harden yourself against God. In essence, you've already been living in a backslidden state that is hurting you spiritually.

Not only that, you also put yourself at great risk physically. There is something called AIDS that is a potential problem with any person who is sexually immoral in this culture.

This certainly isn't to suggest that every person who has AIDS has been sexually immoral. But I do think one of the biggest myths that has been propagated by our culture—especially among our nation's youth—is the concept of "safe sex." It's a blatant lie. I could cite statistic after statistic about how it *isn't* safe, and how there is a great risk factor involved.

A few years ago, I spoke with an individual who had come to our church for counseling. He was terrified because he had been unfaithful to his wife on many occasions, and thought he had AIDS. He had been tested and was waiting for the results. He had to go home and tell his wife what he had done. He had put himself and his marriage at risk while he was out fooling around. What a tragedy.

Have you noticed? People don't think clearly when they

are hooked by lust and sexual sin. It's as if a fog descends over their brains. That's why the Bible warns us to stay away from it, because of its deceptive allure and the power it can exercise over our minds.

It reminds me of a news story I read about a man who lived in England. He had a pet scorpion, which he named Twiggy. Apparently, each night this man would take Twiggy in his hand and give him a little kiss goodnight. One night, to his total surprise, the scorpion stung him on the lip. When the man opened his mouth in shock, the scorpion jumped in and stung him again.

Two things came to mind when I read that story. I won't tell you what the first thing was, because it wouldn't be kind. But the second thing I thought of was that this man underestimated the nature of that creature.

In the same way, we will commit (in our estimation) a "little" sin—something that we don't think is significant. Then we're shocked when it turns around and bites us. We're shocked when it hurts us. We can't believe it happened.

The fact is, no one who is daily walking with Jesus Christ suddenly "falls" into adultery. It's not like some deep pothole in the road that catches you unaware; it's more a cliff-edge that a person keeps straying closer and closer to. Adultery occurs after much denial, self-deception and rationalization. And once you commit adultery, there is vulnerability in your life. The enemy will continue to attack you in this area. You have crossed a line that cannot be uncrossed.

In other words, it's easier to commit adultery a second time when you have done it a first time. It's a bit like breaking a limb. I broke my wrist years ago, and to this day I still feel a weakness there. If I'm not careful, I could break it again. In the same way, there is vulnerability in the life of someone who has already yielded to this devastating sin.

You might say, "Wait a second, Greg. Won't God forgive me?"

Sure He will. But others won't forgive you as quickly. Some never will. And radical measures must be taken to prevent this from ever happening again.

You say, "Well, I'll just marry the person I had the fling with."

Really? But what kind of foundation for marriage would that be? Would you be able to trust a person who has already been unfaithful? Would he or she be able to trust you? Talk about getting off on the wrong foot!

#3: Adultery does incredible damage to your children.

If you break your marriage vows, your position as spiritual leader in your home will be undermined by your own hand. The trust and respect your children had for you will be as eroded as it is with your spouse. What's worse, your children might even follow in your footsteps and repeat your sin in their own lives.

I remember hearing the story of a man who had committed adultery, and his young daughter found out about it. As she grew into a young woman, she started living in a promiscuous way, and he confronted her.

"Honey," he said. "You can't do this. You can't live like this."

"Why not?" she replied. "*You* did."

And what could he reply to that?

Even a spiritual giant like King David had to watch as some of his children repeated his sins of adultery, deception and murder. God forgave David, yes, but he still had to reap the consequences of his rebellion and sin for the rest of his life.

We don't live to ourselves, and we don't die to ourselves. Our decisions in this life—even if we repent of them and find forgiveness—can impact our descendants for generations to come.

#4: Adultery does incredible damage to the church.

The Scripture teaches that when one member of the Body of Christ suffers, we all suffer. When one of us is exalted or God uses one of us in a unique or effective way, we are all blessed. And by the same token, when one of us falls into sin, it touches all of us.

If you are a child of God, you no longer live unto yourself. You don't live on an island. As a result, your actions truly do affect the church as a whole. That is why Paul exhorted the believers in Corinth to remove an immoral man from their midst, because "a little yeast works through the whole batch of dough" (1 Corinthians 5:6, NIV).

Even one immoral person who has seriously compromised God's command and continues to hide his or her sin will have a poisonous, paralyzing impact on the effectiveness of the local church.

#5: Adultery does incredible damage to the cause of Christ.

John, the man who had committed adultery and then wrote me the letter, mentioned that his sin had a direct effect on those with whom he had shared the Lord. He'd had a ministry, and people knew about his stand for Christ. Now all his talk about life in Christ seemed cynical and hypocritical.

The prophet Nathan told something similar to David, after the king had fallen into sin and then covered it up. Nathan said, "By this deed you have given great occasion to the enemies of the LORD to blaspheme" (2 Samuel 12:14).

#6: Adultery is a sin against the Lord.

This should be the primary reason we would want to avoid this sin—but often it's the last thing we think about. You sin against the Lord. You sin against the Savior who loves you. You sin against the One who purchased you with His own blood. You drag His name through the mud. Doesn't that matter to you?

I think what is lacking in the hearts of many Christians today is the fear of God. By "the fear of God," I don't mean the fear of righteous retribution, but the fear of displeasing Him. One of the best definitions I've heard of the fear of God is "a wholesome dread of displeasing Him." In other words, you love God so much that you don't want to do something that would displease Him and bring shame to His name and to the cause of His Kingdom.

Remember in the book of Genesis when young Joseph was being tempted by the wife of Potiphar? This woman was far from subtle. The text gives us this account: "One day, however, no one else was around when he was doing his work inside the house.

She came and grabbed him by his shirt, demanding, 'Sleep with me!'" (Genesis 39:11-12, NLT)

In response, he did what any clear-thinking, red-blooded young man would do under such circumstances. He ran away as quickly as he could! That's what we all ought to do. Flee temptation and don't leave a forwarding address.

What I love, however, was Joseph's statement as to why he didn't want to fall into this sin with the wife of Potiphar. He told her, "How could I ever do such a wicked thing? It would be a great sin against God" (Genesis 39:9, NLT).

Meanwhile, Back in John 8...

Returning to the Lord's encounter with the adulterous woman and her accusers in the temple courtyard, let me suggest that the sin these Pharisees were committing was worse than the sin that she had committed.

You say, "But wait a second. Isn't adultery bad?"

Yes, it is bad. But we have no way of knowing what this woman did or didn't know about the living God and His Word. I think we can safely assume she was not a believer in God.

Why, then, was the sin of these Jewish leaders worse than her sin? Because they *knew better* than she did. So often we're quick to condemn a nonbeliever for their ungodly lifestyle. But have you ever noticed that Jesus saved His most scathing words not for the run-of-the-mill sinners, but for the religious hypocrites of the day?

There are sins of the flesh and sins of the spirit, and one is worse than the other. Second Corinthians 7:1 (NLT) says, "Because we have these promises, dear friends, let us cleanse ourselves from everything that can defile our body or spirit. And let us work toward complete purity because we fear God."

A sin of the spirit is to go against what we know in our hearts to be true.

When Jesus was brought before the pagan ruler Pontius Pilate, the Roman official sentenced Christ to be crucified. Pilate, of course, was wrong when he did that, and it was sin. He should have let the Lord go, because he knew He was innocent. Yet listen to what Jesus said to Pilate in John 19:11 (NLT): "You would have no power over me at all unless it were given to you from above. So the one who brought me to you has the greater sin."

Sometimes someone will ask, "Are some sins worse than others?" According to Jesus, the answer is yes. Who handed Jesus over to Pilate? Caiaphas the high priest. Why was his sin greater? Because Caiaphas was a religious man, a man of faith, a man who spent endless hours poring over the Scriptures, and a man who should have known God.

Caiaphas should have known better. Yet he went against everything he knew in his heart was right, and delivered Jesus to this pagan ruler Pilate, who basically just did his job. It was a greater sin.

That is why we who participate in church, hear the Word of God on a weekly basis, and know biblical truth have to be especially careful. We will be held accountable for what we know. Let's not be guilty of hypocrisy and of condemning others, when we have major cleanup left to do in our own lives, and in our own backyards.

So this guilty, frightened woman was thrown down at the feet of Jesus, and what was He to do? I've already described the dilemma He seemed to be in—a dilemma deliberately planned and implemented by His enemies. Verse 6 tells us that at the very moment a decision was demanded of Him, at a moment when the woman's fate hung in the balance, He knelt down and with His finger and began writing in the dirt.

What did He write?

Great minds of the church have grappled with that question for two millennia, and I won't be able to solve it here. I don't know what He wrote. No one does, and the Bible doesn't tell us. But whatever it was, it cleared the room.

Perhaps He wrote something to this effect: "You're so quick to quote the law to condemn another. Let's see how *you* fare

under its searching light." He might have written the commandments, to remind the people that they had all broken some of
them. Maybe He wrote down the statement, "You shall not commit adultery, but I say to you if you look on a woman with lust in
your heart it is the same."

Maybe He wrote down the name of one of the accusers, and
wrote that man's secret sin underneath it.

Did you know there are no secret sins before God? Secret sin
on Earth is open scandal in heaven, and the Bible says that God
will one day reveal those secrets. Psalm 44:21 declares: "For He
knows the secrets of the heart." Romans 2:16 says: "In that day
when God will judge the secrets of men by Jesus Christ according to my gospel."

The men in the temple courtyard—from the oldest to the
youngest— dropped their rocks, one by one, and slipped away.
Why did the oldest leave first? Because he had the most sins
on his conscience. Soon every one of them had gone, and the
woman was left all alone with Jesus.

In John 8:10, Jesus said, "Woman, where are your accusers?"

In the Greek language of the day, "woman" was a term of
respect and honor. It is the very word Jesus used when speaking
to His mother Mary as He hung on the cross and said, "Woman,
behold your son." It would be like saying "ma'am" or "lady."

I don't know if this girl had ever been referred to as a lady
before. Maybe she didn't think of herself in that way, and certainly others would not have thought of her in those terms.

With great tenderness, Jesus said, "Woman…lady…ma'am…
where are those accusers of yours? Has no one condemned you?"

She said, "No one, Lord."

And Jesus said to her, "Neither do I condemn you; go and sin
no more."

In that moment, Jesus pardoned this woman. How could He
do that, when He knew she was guilty of adultery? Was this leni-
ency on the part of God? Not at all. Jesus knew that in a very short
time He would be going to the cross to die for that sin of immorality

—and for all the rest of her sins and our sins as well.

"Sin No More"

Notice carefully what Jesus said—and what He *didn't* say—here. He said, "Neither do I condemn you; go and sin no more." But He didn't say, "If you go and sin no more, as a result I won't condemn you."

He placed no conditions on His pardon.

Through the years I've met lots of people—even in the church—who are trying so hard to earn the approval of God. They say to themselves, *If I work extra hard this week, read extra chapters in my Bible, pray an extra hour, or talk to a few more people about Jesus, God will approve of me. Then when I come to church on Sunday I will be more right with God. He will smile on me.*

But that's not the way it works. You already have the approval and smile of God, and it's not because of what you've done or what you do. It is because of what Jesus did already on your behalf. The Bible says that He has made me "accepted in the Beloved" (Ephesians 1:6).

There was no way I could ever earn His approval. But because of what Christ did for me, essentially standing in my place and paying the price for my sin, God sees me through Jesus. As a result, He approves of me, receives me, and forgives me.

In recognition of that, I should "go and sin no more." I should go and seek to live a godly life. Not to earn God's approval, but rather with the grateful knowledge that I already have it.

When Jesus said "go and sin no more" to this woman, He didn't mean "go and live a perfect life." He knew she wouldn't. He knows we won't. If that were the standard for qualifying, none of us would ever make it. We will sin and fall short of His righteous standards. As James reminds us, "We all stumble in many ways" (James 3:2).

No, the idea Jesus conveyed to the woman in the temple courtyard was more like this: "Dear lady, I am pardoning you right now. I am forgiving you of every sin you have ever done.

Now you need to stop living in this lifestyle of sin. Turn away from it from this moment forward."

I think in that minute she believed in Jesus Christ, and put her faith in Him. She looked at Jesus and thought, *I've never seen anyone like this before. No one has ever looked at me like this before. No man has ever treated me with this kind of respect before. I believe in Him.*

Belief can happen that quickly. I have watched conversion take place before my very eyes. You have, too. When someone walks forward in an evangelistic crusade? Yes, but I don't think everyone who responds to a public call for commitment to Christ is converted at the moment they pray with the evangelist. I think many of them are converted before they even get to the meeting or to the church, because of the faithful witness of believers in their lives. They've just been waiting to make it public.

I've seen others who have believed in the midst of a message. As a pastor, I can look out at the audience and often spot the nonbelievers. I don't know exactly how to explain it; there's just something that sets them apart. And I've seen God work in their hearts as they hear the Gospel message and—perhaps for the first time—actually understand it.

That's how I think it was for this woman in John 8. Jesus said, "Has no one condemned you?" She replied, "No one, Lord." And in that moment Jesus truly became her Lord and Savior.

It was like that with one of the thieves who had been hung on a cross next to Jesus'. Initially, that condemned felon joined in the chorus of mockers who said, "Let Him save Himself, if He is the Son of God." But then Jesus gave His first of seven statements from the cross, when He said to His Father, "Father, forgive them, for they do not know what they do."

In a moment, in a flash, that thief believed. He turned to Jesus and said, "Lord, remember me when You come into Your kingdom."

Belief can happen that quickly, as I believe it did with this woman whom Jesus pardoned. In extending His forgiveness to her, Jesus gave her three wonderful promises.

Three Promises

#1. Her sins could be forgotten.

When Jesus said, "Go and sin no more," He was already speaking to this woman's future. Her past was no longer an issue. Similarly, in Jeremiah 31:34, the Lord says, "I will forgive their iniquity and I will remember their sin no more."

When God forgives, God forgets. And we should not choose to remember what God has chosen to forget. Sometimes we will find ourselves inclined to dig up our old sins and feel condemned all over again. There is no need for that; those sins have been forgiven and the debt has been canceled. They are under the blood of Jesus Christ, and have been forgotten by God.

I love the word "justified" that is used so many times in the New Testament. What does it mean that you and I have been justified? The word justified could be translated to say "just as if it had never happened."

That is what God does for you. He forgives your sins and He forgets them. As Corrie ten Boom once said, "God takes our sins, throws them into the sea of forgetfulness, and posts a sign that says, 'No fishing allowed.'"[28]

#2. She did not need to fear the judgment day.

"Neither do I condemn you," Jesus said. And the Bible tells us in Romans 8:1, "There is therefore now no condemnation to those who are in Christ Jesus." The devil may try to condemn you, but it's all deception, smoke and mirrors, because there is no condemnation to be found. Why? Because the guilt and sentence of death that should rightfully have fallen on you and me was placed on Jesus when He hung on the cross.

#3. She had new power to face her problems.

"Go and sin no more."

He was essentially saying to her, "I am giving you new power. You don't have to live that way any longer. I am giving you the strength not to fall in this area again."

Maybe you're an individual who struggles with sexual sin and impurity—whether pornography, mental fantasies, or in actual unfaithfulness to your spouse.

The first thing you must do is to stop rationalizing, stop lying to yourself, admit that this is a sin before God, and repent, breaking your old patterns and habits and refusing to return to them.

We all live in the same corrupt, morally broken world that brims with snares and seductions. Nevertheless, there are places and people we can avoid to keep ourselves from temptation. The best way to deal with sin, especially lustful sin, is to starve it. Simply refuse to feed those impure and destructive thoughts, and stay away from anything that might encourage them.

If you are in sexual sin, you need to know that it's a soul-destroying way to live, and grieves the Spirit of God. God will forgive you, but you need to stop these thoughts and actions immediately and confess your sin to the Lord. And He will say to you, "Neither do I condemn you. Go and sin no more."

Perhaps someone you know has fallen into this sin. You need to reach out to him or her. I know it's difficult, awkward and uncomfortable. First of all, they will probably lie about it. (People generally do.) Then again, they may try to rationalize and excuse what they are doing, and tell you why it's okay.

Here is where you have to be strong, for the sake of your friend or loved one. The Bible says, "Faithful are the wounds of a friend, but the kisses of an enemy are deceitful" (Proverbs 27:6).

You don't have to solve all of their problems at this point or preach a sermon. Your responsibility as a friend is to lovingly but firmly say, "No, it's not okay. What you are doing is wrong. Brother, sister, I love you and you have to stop doing this, because you will bring the judgment of God upon yourself. You don't understand the damage this is doing. Stop doing it."

The object, remember, is to restore—and to help that individual back on their feet again. To help them break free from that lifestyle. As I said earlier, one day it could be you or me.

John 8 assures us that Jesus didn't leave this woman in her sin and condemnation. She had fallen down and lay in the dust, but He helped her to her feet, and sent her out in newness of life.

He will do the same for your fallen friend…or for you.

Questions for Discussion

1. *"In her sin, humiliation and dread, she had been brought to the feet of Jesus, and what could have been the worst day of her life became the very best day of her life."*

Reflect on the circumstances that ultimately brought you to Jesus Christ—or brought you back to Him after a long time of wandering away. Talk about the paradox of how the worst circumstances of life can end up being the best circumstances of life, because of the way God steps in.

2. *"Those who are the quickest to quote Scripture in order to condemn others are frequently the guiltiest of all. ... The biggest fault-finders and nitpickers are often guilty of worse sin in their own lives."*

Read again Matthew 5:3-5. How can we find the balance between rightfully confronting loved ones who are in danger of falling into sin, and remembering that we too have faults and failures in our own lives?

3. According to James 6:1-2, what should we do if we know of a fellow believer who has compromised his or her standards and fallen into the sin of adultery? What does this passage say our principle objective must be?

4. What does James means when he adds, *"considering yourself lest you also be tempted"*?

5. Greg notes: *"Lies and deception in one area of life tend to leach, like toxic sludge, into every other area of life. In other words, very soon you won't just be living a lie, you will be a lie."*

What are some very small lies we might use—that might lead us to justify dishonesty in other areas of our lives? Why do we need to confront these sins in ourselves before they take root?

6. Following Greg's chance encounter with "John," the man who was just about to commit adultery, John later wondered if Greg's happening along at that moment was God giving him once last chance to turn away from terrible sin. What warnings, nudges or obstacles has God used in your life at various times to turn you in a different direction and protect you from some foolish course of action? Reflect on God's desire and provision to protect His children, as set forth in Matthew 6:13 and Hebrews 10:13.

7. Greg writes: *"To even get to this place where you're willing to commit adultery means that you've had to harden yourself against God. In essence, you've already been living in a backslidden state that is hurting you spiritually."*

Read Hebrews 3:12-13, and then answer this question: Why is it important for believers to encourage one another daily to walk with God and turn away from sin? According to these verses, what might happen to the one who withdraws from the exhortation and encouragement of fellow believers?

8. Greg writes: *"People don't think clearly when they are hooked by lust and sexual sin. It's as if a fog descends over their brains. That's why the Bible warns us to stay away from it, because of its deceptive allure and the power it can exercise over our minds."*

Can you think of any examples where you have seen this happen? How does Proverbs 6:32-33 summarize this point?

9. *"Adultery is not like some deep pothole in the road that catches you unaware; it's more a cliff-edge that a person keeps straying closer and closer to."*

Discuss the word picture above. Do you agree with it? How might people justify the practice of walking closer and closer to the cliff-edge—or even peering over the brink?

10. Christians who choose to engage in immorality sometimes feel like they are only hurting themselves. Paul, however, exhorted the believers in Corinth to remove an immoral man from their midst, because "a little yeast works through the whole batch of dough" (1 Corinthians 5:6, NIV).

What did Paul mean by that? How does the sin of one member of Christ's Body affect the whole?

CHAPTER 9
Standing Strong Against Temptation

God blesses the people who patiently endure testing. Afterward they will receive the crown of life that God has promised to those who love him.
–James 1:12, NLT

We live in a culture today that is obsessed with sex—before marriage, outside of marriage, and in almost every perverse form imaginable.

It just seems to get worse all the time. If historians were to look back at our time—at our movies, TV shows, magazines, and billboards—they would certainly have to conclude that this was a sex-obsessed culture.

Of course, none of this should surprise us.

Jesus Himself said that in the last days would be filled with wickedness— comparable to the days of Noah, and the days of Lot.

When I return the world will be as indifferent to the things of God as the people were in Noah's day. They ate and drank and married-everything just as usual right up to the day when Noah went into the ark and the flood came and destroyed them all.

And the world will be as it was in the days of Lot: people went about their daily business—eating and drinking, buying and selling, farming and building—until the morning Lot left Sodom. Then fire and brimstone rained down from heaven and destroyed them all. Yes, it will be 'business as usual' right up to the hour of my return. (Luke 17:26-30, TLB)

Both of those eras in human history were characterized by unbridled sexual perversion.

Of course, all of these things undermine marriages and

families. In the last chapter we discussed adultery. It has spread throughout our society, and we see its effects all around. But how widespread is it? According to some statistics, 50 to 60 percent of all men have had extramarital affairs,[29] and nearly 70% of all married men under 40 expect to have an extramarital relationship.[30] But if you think this problem is unique to men, think again. The women are catching up. Unfaithfulness on the part of women toward their husbands is now almost equal with that of the men.

Are you committing adultery? Are you planning to? Have you been thinking about it? Considering the statistics, it's entirely possible. I just want you to think for a few moments about the repercussions and the damage this sin can bring to you, your spouse and your family. So significant is the sin of adultery that it made the top ten—the Ten Commandments, that is. "You shall not commit adultery," God says (Exodus 20:14). Then He expands on it: "You shall not covet your neighbor's wife" (v. 17).

Why did God give us commandments like these? It was for our own protection, because He knows what devastation it can bring.

The Bible asks, "Can a man take fire to his bosom, and his clothes not be burned?" (Proverbs 6:27) The answer, of course, is no. If you scoop red-hot coals onto your chest, you'll soon understand the consequences. A fire can get out of control so easily. And so can lust! You think, I *can contain this. I can handle this. This is no problem.* Then suddenly the burning embers of lust are blowing over your life and you've lost all control.

What happened? You took fire into your bosom, or into your heart or into your life, and you were burned. You were one of the many who thought they could handle it.

That's what Samson deluded himself into thinking. He thought, *What is this lady Delilah going to do to me? I'm the mighty Samson. I can tear apart a young lion with my bare hands. I can kill a thousand Philistines with the jawbone of a donkey. What impact can one little woman have on me?*

But the devil was sly. He knew he could never bring Samson down on the battlefield, so he brought him down in the bedroom. It was a sneak attack through this woman Delilah, whose name, ironically, means "delicate."

She began to break down Samson's resolve and resistance until he finally confessed to her the secret of his supernatural strength (see Judges 16:16–21). If only he could have come to his senses and realized he was falling into a trap.

It's the same thing with lust. It's devastating, and it destroys thousands of marriages today, as well ruining the lives of countless young people. Aside from the moral and emotional implications, it's also killing people and ravaging lives through sexually transmitted diseases.

"Don't Be Naïve"

You might be thinking, *Greg, did you have to devote two chapters to sexual sin? I really don't need to hear this. I would never fall into this sin. My spouse and I have an ideal marriage. I can't imagine any circumstances in which I would ever be unfaithful.*

I remember listening to an interview with a man who had written some Christian books on the family. This man had boasted to his friends, "If I ever fall into sin, I guarantee it will not be adultery. Anything but. I love my wife so much that it would never happen to me."

Do you know what happened? You guessed it. This man fell into the sin of adultery, and ended up doing the very things he said he would never, ever do. He concluded the interview with these highly significant words: *"An unguarded strength is a double weakness."*

How true! Whenever we say things like, "I would never fall into that sin," we're already on very thin ice. It's almost like issuing a challenge to Satan and his demons to attack us in a given area of our lives.

And that would be very, very foolish.

In 1 Corinthians 10:12 (PHILLIPS), we read: "So let the man

who feels sure of his standing today be careful that he does not fall tomorrow."

The Message Bible paraphrases the verse like this:

Don't be so naïve and self-confident. You're not exempt. You could fall flat on your face as easily as anyone else. Forget about self-confidence; it's useless. Cultivate God-confidence.

Any of us are capable of committing any sin.

Don't ever forget that.

You are capable of doing terrible, unthinkable things, and so am I. As the prophet Jeremiah warns us: "The heart is deceitful above all things, and desperately wicked" (Jeremiah 17:9).

Over in the New Testament, the Apostle Paul declares:

I know I am rotten through and through so far as my old sinful nature is concerned. No matter which way I turn I can't make myself do right. I want to but I can't. When I want to do good, I don't; and when I try not to do wrong, I do it anyway. (Romans 7:18-19, TLB)

That doesn't mean I will actually do all these sinful things, but it certainly means the *potential* is always there. We dare not let down our guard.

Peter warned his listeners:

Be well balanced (temperate, sober of mind), be vigilant and cautious at all times; for that enemy of yours, the devil, roams around like a lion roaring [in fierce hunger], seeking someone to seize upon and devour. (1 Peter 5:8, AMPLIFIED)

If I allow temptation to infiltrate my life and my old nature to prevail, I could fall, just as surely as a fire will spread if gasoline is poured on it. But if I take practical steps and precautions to guard myself and to stay close to the Lord, then I don't have to fall.

The Lesson of Balaam

In warning believers about fornication, Paul said, "Nor let us commit sexual immorality, as some of them did, and in one day twenty-three thousand fell" (1 Corinthians 10:8). Paul refers here to the book of Numbers and the story of the greedy prophet, Balaam, who was a sort of "prophet for hire."

When Balak, the king of the Moabites, wanted the Israelites defeated, he thought that finding a prophet to curse them and bring God's judgment on them would be much easier than having to defeat them on the battlefield.

I don't know where he found a prophet like Balaam. Maybe he looked in the Moab Yellow Pages under "profit," because that seems to be all Balaam was interested in. Whatever the case, he secured Balaam's services, told him to go and curse Israel, and offered a very generous contract to do it. No problem, Balaam said. So he went out to curse Israel, but God spoke to Balaam and told him not to curse Israel, but to bless them.

This didn't exactly endear him to Balak. He hadn't hired a top-gun prophet to bless the people; he hired him to curse them. Still, Balaam was determined to somehow find a way to get this money. He went on his way to do what God had told him not to do, and in one of the Bible's most attention-grabbing narratives, his donkey spoke to him. You would think that would have been enough for Balaam right then and there. But he persisted and eventually devised a plan.

"I'll tell you what, Balak," the reckless prophet counseled. "I can't curse the Israelites. God has told me not to. But I have an idea. If you can get some of your young, sensual Moabite women to entice these young Israelite men to go into their tents and have sexual relations with them, that is a way you can get them to worship the false gods. If these Israelite men actually enter the tents and engage in this idolatry, this will bring God's wrath on the people and He will judge them."

"Good idea," Balak said, and he enlisted the women to do the work. So the young women went out, and it was a success—depending on how you look at it. The story is recorded in Numbers 25, where we read,

> *Now Israel remained in Acacia Grove, and the people began to commit harlotry with the women of Moab. They invited the people to the sacrifices of their gods, and the people ate and bowed down to their gods. So Israel was joined to Baal of Peor, and the anger of the Lord was aroused against Israel. Then the Lord said to Moses,*

"Take all the leaders of the people and hang the offenders before the Lord, out in the sun, that the fierce anger of the Lord may turn away from Israel." (vv. 1–4)

These weren't the first people to be destroyed by immorality, and they won't be the last. So Paul was now bringing this example before the people he was speaking to: the church of Corinth, and to believers who are living in the last days. The Corinthian believers were a bit smug. They somehow thought they would never fall into sexual sin or idolatry. This is why Paul framed these words in the way he did.

Ironically, immorality was rampant in Corinth in Paul's day. In fact, towering above the ruins of old Corinth is a 2000-foot mountain fortress called Acrocorinth. Situated at the top of that mountain was the Temple of Aphrodite, the Greek goddess of fertility, and as many as a thousand priestesses, or prostitutes, working for the temple, carried on their immoral activities in worship of this pagan deity.

It is said that the prostitutes from this temple would go into the city of Corinth wearing specially designed sandals that left the words "follow me" imprinted on the sand.[31]

Many citizens of Corinth did just that. They followed the prostitutes to the temple and committed sexual immorality as well as idolatry.

I think the same invitation to commit sexual immorality is being extended to us today by way of the media's constant bombardment of our culture with sex. The message is hard to miss: "Follow me."

Watch Your Step

Usually the steps that lead to sexual immorality, including adultery, are numerous. It happens over a period of time, generally beginning in the area of the imagination, and then leading up to the act itself.

We see this in the life of one man who committed adultery and paid the price for it in the years to come. His name was David. Sadly, when you think of David's life, two names come up that sum up his whole story—David and Goliath, and David and Bathsheba. One represents his greatest triumph, while the other represents his greatest defeat.

I've referenced David and Bathsheba a couple of times already in this book, but I'd like to highlight an additional point or two. The incident began in the spring, when the Bible tells us that kings were going out to battle. All of the kings, except David, who was taking some time off. He was out strolling on his patio when he looked down and saw a beautiful woman named Bathsheba bathing herself. Now, he couldn't have avoided that first look—and sometimes you wonder if Bathsheba allowed herself to be in a place where she would be seen by David, knowing she was within view.

Maybe or maybe not. One thing we do know is that the Bible never points the finger at her. David was the culprit in this case. He couldn't have avoided that first look, but the second one is probably what got him into trouble.

He then began to devise a plan in which he could have Bathsheba. Misusing his authority and position as king, he commanded her to be brought up to his chambers. He had sexual relations with her, and she became pregnant. But instead of confessing his sin to God, he tried to cover up what he had done. So he sent word that Bathsheba's husband, Uriah, who was serving David in his army, was to be brought back to be with his wife. David wanted to cover it up.

Uriah was brought back, but David hadn't reckoned on the fact of this brave soldier's rock-solid integrity. How could he have the pleasure of being with his wife when his fellow soldiers were out risking their lives on the battlefield. In spite of what the king said, Uriah determined to sleep outside his own house that night.

David should have stopped right there.

I think it was a moment of grace, a moment where he might have caught himself and saved himself from falling into still deeper sin. It was as though God was putting an obstacle in his path, trying to warn him. But David persisted. He got Uriah drunk, then sent him in to be with his wife. Again, Uriah would not have relations with his wife.

So David ordered his commander to have Uriah sent to the front lines, where he was killed in the heat of battle. Then, without wasting much time, David took Bathsheba into his home and married her.

David may have thought he pulled it off, but it doesn't work that way. The Bible says, "He who covers his sins will not prosper" (Proverbs 28:13). For twelve terrible months, David lived out of harmony and fellowship with the God he loved so much. He later wrote in the psalms about what it's like to live out of fellowship with God when there is unconfessed sin, and his words still ring so true to any who have ever been in a similar position.

Take a few moments and ponder David's anguished words:

> When I kept it all inside,
> my bones turned to powder,
> my words became daylong groans.
> The pressure never let up;
> all the juices of my life dried up.
> (Psalm 32:3-4, THE MESSAGE)

If you are engaged in unconfessed sin right now, be it in action or even in the realm of the imagination, then you know what David is talking about. You know the destruction that that sin can bring. That is why the Bible tells us in Proverbs 6:32, "But the man who commits adultery is an utter fool, for he destroys his own soul" (NLT). If you choose to commit adultery, then you are choosing self-destruction.

Don't Let It Happen to You

So what steps can we take to prevent this devastating sin of sexual immorality? What can we do to build a wall of protection around our lives and around our marriages?

First, walk with God.

It's simple, but true. If a husband or wife is truly walking with God, it will give him or her the power to stand strong against tempta-

tion and say, like Joseph, "How then can I do this great wickedness, and sin against God?" It was David's failure to do this that
made him vulnerable to the temptations he faced. You'd think
that David, "the man after God's own heart," would have stopped
himself after looking at Bathsheba, and said, "What am I thinking?
How could I do such a thing? How could I sin against the God
who loves me and has cared for me through all of these years?"

But David evidently hadn't been walking with God for some
time, because when the temptation came, it seems he didn't give
the Lord a second thought.

Job said, "I have made a covenant with my eyes; why then
should I look upon a young woman?" (Job 31:1). Job said, "I am
guarding myself. I am careful as to what I look at." On the same
subject, Jesus said,

> You have heard that it was said to those of old, 'You shall not
> commit adultery.' But I say to you that whoever looks at a woman
> to lust for her has already committed adultery with her in his
> heart. If your right eye causes you to sin, pluck it out and cast
> it from you; for it is more profitable for you that one of your
> members perish, than for your whole body to be cast into hell.
> (Matthew 5:27–29)

When Jesus used the phrase "looks at a woman," He wasn't
just talking about just seeing her. Nor was He talking about being
exposed to something you didn't want to be exposed to. The fact
is, we can't always control our environment and what's thrown in
front of us—particularly in our sex-saturated media world. But
again, Jesus wasn't speaking about a casual glance here. What
He referred to was deliberate, continual act of looking. In this
usage, the idea is not of an incidental or involuntarily glance, but
an intentional and repeated gazing with the express purpose of
lusting. I might also add that this statement doesn't apply to men
only. It also applies to women looking lustfully at men.

So what this refers to here is a person who actually goes out
of his or her way to look at someone to lust after them. This
could happen in real life, and it could also happen via computer,
where a person deliberately downloads provocative, lustful

images to stare at.

So here was Jesus' solution: "If your right eye causes you to sin, pluck it out and cast it from you" (Matthew 5:29).

You say, "Isn't that a little radical?" Yes, but it's not *literal*. If we took this literally, there wouldn't be many people left with a right eye. Obviously Jesus wasn't speaking literally, because if you pluck out your right eye, you could still lust with your left. So we need to understand the culture of the time, which is often helpful in interpreting various passages of Scripture.

In the Jewish culture, the right hand represented a person's best and most precious faculties, and the right eye represented one's best vision. What Jesus was saying, in essence, is that you should be willing to give up whatever is necessary to keep from falling into sin. Whatever steps you have to take that would prevent you from falling morally or spiritually, *take them*.

If there is something in your life, whether it's a relationship or something you're doing that causes you to commit this sin of looking with lust, then you need to stop. Now. *Looking always leads to doing.* If it isn't stopped at some point, then sooner or later, you'll be tired of just looking and want to start doing. That's why it needs to be nipped in the bud—in the realm of your mind.

The Bible says, "Walk in the Spirit, and you shall not fulfill the lust of the flesh" (Galatians 5:16). The best defense is a good offense. So walk with God.

Second, walk with your spouse.

In other words, enjoy a close and intimate friendship and romance with your wife or husband. Friendship and companionship between spouses is at the very foundation of a marriage. We talked about this earlier in the book, but I can't emphasize it enough. Your spouse should be your best friend.

Building on that warm and affectionate friendship, keep the romance alive in your marriage. Cultivate it. If the romance is dying, then get it back and throw some more logs on the fire. Do what you can to rekindle it again.

Take care to sexually fulfill one other. The Bible tells you,

"Drink water from your own cistern, and running water from your own well" (Proverbs 5:15). Find fulfillment in your marriage relationship as husband and wife, as God has created you and has blessed that union. Guard this intimate area of your love relationship, and don't let anything keep you from fulfilling one another's desires.

Third, don't walk in the counsel of the ungodly.

Avoid at all costs any relationship or friendship that could cause you to fall.

If you find yourself in a questionable relationship with someone of the opposite sex right now, if you're flirting and playing around, then it's time to throw on the brakes. "Oh, it's innocent," you might say. But please listen—you never know what it could lead to. Avoid this danger at all costs. Scripture tells us to avoid even the appearance of evil (see 1 Thessalonians 5:22, KJV).

Count the cost. Remember some of the warnings we've been looking at. These strong cautions, along with an intense love for God and your spouse, can see you through the rough waters of sexual temptation.

Temptation will be around as long as we live. But we don't have to fall into it if we take the steps God has given us. And if you have fallen into it, *stop*. Repent. Turn around. Don't take one more step in the wrong direction. Thank God there is forgiveness, and learn from your mistakes.

Let's not forget the words of 1 Corinthians 10:13,

No temptation has overtaken you except such as is common to man; but God is faithful, who will not allow you to be tempted beyond what you are able, but with the temptation will also make the way of escape, that you may be able to bear it.

This clearly tells us that God won't give us more than we can handle. He won't let us be tempted above our capacity to resist. So you don't have to give in to that impure thought. You don't have to give in to that sinful idea. You don't have to visit those questionable sites on the Internet.

You can't stop yourself from being tempted, but remember

this: The tempter needs the cooperation of the temptee! We are tempted, the Bible says, when we are drawn away by our own lusts and enticed (see James 1:14). So while it's true that temptation can be strong, it won't overpower you if you refuse to cooperate with it.

As has been said, you can't stop a bird from flying over your head, but you can stop it from building a nest in your hair. It's not a sin to be tempted. Jesus was tempted, after all. But it is a sin to give in to temptation.

Don't forget that God is always ready to help you in this struggle against your old nature. Psalm 46:1 reminds us that "God is our refuge and strength, a very present help in trouble." In the Lord's Prayer, Jesus leads us to pray, "And lead us not into temptation, but deliver us from the evil one." He wouldn't have given us that prayer if He didn't mean for us to use it. Seek God's face and pray to be delivered from the presence and power of Satan's lures, traps and schemes.

In the Garden of Gethsemane, Jesus said to His men, "Watch and pray so that you will not fall into temptation. The spirit is willing, but the body is weak" (Matthew 26:41, NIV). That's still wonderful counsel for you and me…every day of our lives.

The fact is, when it comes to devastating sexual sin, you *do* have a choice in the matter.

As Moses once said to the people of Israel, *"Choose life."*

Questions for Discussion

1. Read Proverbs 6:27-29. What does this passage say to an individual who says about lust, "I can handle it. I can play with it just a little without doing much harm"?

2. Discuss the danger of considering a sin like adultery and saying to yourself, *It could never happen to me. I could never do anything like that.*

3. Greg quoted a man who had sworn it "could never happen to me," only to fall into adultery after all. Later, the man wrote: *"An unguarded strength is a double weakness."* What does that statement mean to you?

4. The Message Bible paraphrases 1 Corinthians 10:12 with these words: *"Don't be so naïve and self-confident. You're not exempt. You could fall flat on your face as easily as anyone else. Forget about self-confidence; it's useless. Cultivate God-confidence."*

Forget self-confidence? That certainly goes against the grain of our culture, doesn't it? Contrast self-confidence with God-confidence. Why do we need God-confidence to stand against temptation and sin?

5. The Apostle Peter writes: *"Be self-controlled and alert. Your enemy the devil prowls around like a roaring lion looking for someone to devour. Resist him, standing firm in the faith, because you know that your brothers throughout the world are undergoing the same kind of sufferings"* (1 Peter 5:8-9, NIV).

What practical steps can we take to make sure we walk through our day "self-controlled and alert," and ready to resist Satan's attacks?

6. Read Psalm 32:1-5. What did David experience when he tried to cover over his sins, rather than dealing with them before God? What was the result when he finally decided to open up his life for God's inspection and cleansing?

7. How would daily praying David's prayer in Psalm 139:23-24 keep us from falling into destructive sins?

8. Read Matthew 5:27-29. Why does Jesus use such a drastic word picture here? What is He saying about those things/places/people/habits in our lives that continually trip us up and lead us into sin?

9. The Bible says, "Walk in the Spirit, and you shall not fulfill the lust of the flesh" (Galatians 5:16).

There's an old football expression that says, "The best defense is a good offense." How would you apply that saying to walking with God and seeking to avoid sin?

10. Read 1 Corinthians 10:13. What is God's promise? What is our responsibility?

CHAPTER 10
The Incredible Power of Words

Words kill, words give life; They're either poison or fruit—you choose.
—Proverbs 18:21, THE MESSAGE

A few years ago, Cathe and I were invited to stay at a cabin in Virginia that belonged to some friends. This cabin didn't have any heat to speak of, except for a fireplace and a little furnace downstairs that had to be fed a regular diet of logs.

"I know this might sound stupid," I told the owners, "but I don't know how to build a fire very well."

"Well," they said, "the first thing you have to do is go out and get some kindling."

"Okay. Where do you buy that?"

"You don't buy it," they told me. "You go find it. Kindling is the little sticks and branches that you use to start the fire."

"Oh."

Then they showed me the proper way to start a fire, and pointed out that once the fireplace is filled with enough ash, I would need to scoop it out, put it into a metal bucket, and then keep the bucket on a concrete surface so all of the embers will cool down.

"Be careful to make sure they've all cooled down," they cautioned. "They do stay quite live for a period of time."

It was freezing cold outside, and since our California blood is so thin, we had to keep the fireplace and furnace going nonstop.

I would get up at 3 a.m. to add more wood to the fires. After a while, however, the fireplace was filled with ashes. I got out the shovel and filled the bucket all the way to the brim. After waiting for what I thought had been a couple of days, I decided it was time to empty the bucket.

It was late at night, and Cathe was already asleep. I went outside in my PJs and slippers, took the bucket of ash, and pitched it out into the forest.

Looking back now, it was one of those moments where it seemed like everything was moving in slow motion. Much to my horror, I saw, in the ash, these little burning embers. Immediately, small fires were starting—three fires right off the bat. I started picking up the live, burning embers with my hands and throwing them up on the driveway.

Then a breeze came along and more little fires erupted. I ran into the cabin to look for some kind of bucket and found one that looked slightly larger than a drinking glass. Quickly filling it with water, I poured it on one of my fires, and ran back again for more water.

You'd better believe that I was calling on the Lord for help. I thought I would burn the whole forest down—and Cathe and myself with it—but fortunately, that didn't happen. The rest of the night, however, I kept looking out through the window, thinking I would see a huge forest fire erupt any moment.

That experience reminded me of the truth of the statement James made when he said, "So also, the tongue is a small thing, but what enormous damage it can do. A tiny spark can set a great forest on fire" (James 3:5, NLT).

How true that is. More people have died by the power of the tongue than by any other weapon humanity has ever devised.

The World's Most Dangerous Weapon

Today, manufacturers put warning labels on their products so we won't do something stupid. They're trying to protect themselves from potential lawsuits. Consider all of the safety standards we have in place for everything from automobile emissions to gun control. Yet the most dangerous weapon and the most toxic pollutant is left unchecked: the tongue.

We desperately need to learn how to control it, and especially in our marriages. If we were brutally honest, I'm sure we could look back on this past year (or maybe even the past week) and admit we have said a few things to our spouse that we've lived to regret.

Dedicated to God, our tongues can be a powerful force for good in our marriages and in the lives of those around us. But left unchecked, especially when yielded to the enemy, the tongue is the most destructive weapon on the face of the Earth. It has the terrible potential to tear down marriages and destroy lives.

As followers of Jesus Christ, we know a lot about certain sins we should avoid. We know that we aren't supposed to lie. We know that we aren't supposed to steal. We know that we aren't supposed to be immoral. We go out of our way to avoid things that would drag us down spiritually.

Yet one thing we are warned about many times in Scripture is often left unchecked among believers. It is also an area that is grossly neglected by many husbands and wives…and that is *thinking about what we say*.

For example, we would never dream of taking out a knife and thrusting it into our husband or wife. Yet we can wound our partner deeply with a few carelessly spoken words. These are spiritual wounds, and they can leave scars that last every bit as long as physical wounds.

Most of us can remember hurtful words and taunts from the earliest days of childhood. Years and decades may roll by, but simply recalling those harsh or degrading words has the power to bring pain to the soul.

The book of James offers some wise observations about the tongue:

> *We all stumble in many ways. If anyone is never at fault in what he says, he is a perfect man, able to keep his whole body in check.*

When we put bits into the mouths of horses to make them obey us, we can turn the whole animal. Or take ships as an example. Although they are so large and are driven by strong winds, they are steered by a very small rudder wherever the pilot wants to go.

Likewise the tongue is a small part of the body, but it makes great boasts. Consider what a great forest is set on fire by a small spark.

The tongue also is a fire, a world of evil among the parts of the body. It corrupts the whole person, sets the whole course of his life on fire, and is itself set on fire by hell.

All kinds of animals, birds, reptiles and creatures of the sea are being tamed and have been tamed by man, but no man can tame the tongue. It is a restless evil, full of deadly poison.

With the tongue we praise our Lord and Father, and with it we curse men, who have been made in God's likeness. Out of the same mouth come praise and cursing. My brothers, this should not be. (James 3:2–10, NIV)

James tells us that the tongue is like a fire, like a bit, like a beast, and like a poison, among other things.

Take James' example of the bit. We can make a large, powerful horse turn around—almost midstride—and go wherever we want by means of a small bit in its mouth. A few years ago at the Rose Parade, I watched a man riding a buffalo down the street. He had a saddle on it and a bit in its mouth. It was amazing to me that this rider could control a massive beast with a tiny bit. Just as a bit controls a horse (or a buffalo, in some cases), we are controlled by our words.

One word can virtually set the course that your life takes. Saying "I do" to a partner in marriage means a lifetime of commitment. Saying "I won't" to the temptation of an extramarital affair could save that marriage from destruction. Of course, saying "I will" to Jesus Christ will forever change your eternal destiny.

Our tongues control us. What we say affects what we do. It also profoundly affects our marriages.

The tongue is a small thing, but what an enormous amount of damage it can do. The mere two ounces of mucous membrane in our mouths can do so much evil or so much good.

Think of those who have dedicated their words to darkness and to the devil. There was Adolf Hitler, for example, who, through his demonic rhetoric, led an entire nation down the pathway to hell, and caused the useless and needless slaughter of countless people. This is what a tongue dedicated to the devil can do.

Then we have the example of someone who has dedicated his words to God: Billy Graham. The result has been millions of people who have given their lives to Jesus Christ.

So to whom—and to what—are you dedicating your words? Are you dedicating them to God, and toward the goal of building up your husband, your wife, your family, and other people God has placed in your life?

Take Time to Listen

James 1:19 is a verse I think we should post where we can see it on a daily basis: "My dear brothers and sisters, be quick to listen, slow to speak, and slow to get angry" (NLT). The problem is that too often we are swift to speak, slow to listen, and quick to get angry!

What does it mean to be "quick to listen"?

I think it implies taking time to hear someone out. Have you ever made a statement to your spouse or your children based on an incorrect understanding of what was happening, because you didn't take the time to hear them out? You were quick to make a snap judgment, and just as quick to sound off about it. That's why the Bible says, "What a shame, what folly, to give advice before listening to the facts!" (Proverbs 18:13, NLT)

In our era of instant messaging and ten-second sound bites, we find it difficult to slow down, be still and truly *listen*. But the Bible says we need to be quick about that. We need to be quick to listen—and especially quick to hear what our husband or wife has to say.

After 38 years of marriage, Cathe knows what I mean when I say certain words. She discerns things by the tone of my voice. She is "quick to hear," and that is vitally important in a marriage.

A Failure to Communicate

One of the more famous Hollywood lines emerged from the

early Paul Newman movie *Cool Hand Luke*. Just after hitting the escaped prisoner Luke with a baton, sending him sprawling, the prison guard drawls, "What we got here [pause] … is a failure to communicate."

Most communication breakdowns will never be as extreme as that, but in a marriage, "failure to communicate" can be especially hurtful. One husband was overheard saying to his wife, "Honey, what do you mean we don't communicate? Just yesterday I e-mailed you a reply to the message you left on my voice mail!" That's communication for you.

Still, it's amazing how a husband and wife who are trying to communicate can talk right past each other. What a wife says may translate into something entirely different for her husband. Likewise, what he says may mean something else to his wife. When a couple is driving somewhere and they get lost, she will say, "Let's ask for directions." But he hears, "You're not a man."

When she says, "Can I have the remote control?", he hears, "Let's watch something that will bore you beyond belief!"

She tells him, "You need to get in touch with your feelings." He hears, *"Blah, blah, blah."*

She asks, "Are you listening to me?" He hears, *"Blah, blah, blah, blah, blah."*

She says, "I'd like to redecorate." He hears, *"Let's take our money and flush it down the toilet."*

What we have here is a failure to communicate! But we have to keep trying, don't we?

Not only should we be quick to listen, James tells us, but we should also be slow to get angry. As Proverbs 29:11 tells us, "A fool gives full vent to anger, but a wise person quietly holds it back" (NLT). Don't let anger control your life. Don't let it have a place in your marriage.

I heard about a husband and wife who, as newlyweds, decided to put into practice Ephesians 4:26, which says, "Be angry, and do not sin: do not let the sun go down on your wrath." So they determined never to go to bed mad at each other. Thirty years later, someone asked the husband how it worked out. He replied, "Pretty well, but sometimes it was a little rough sitting up all night."

Yet there are certain people who are always mad about something. They never seem to be happy unless they are mad. They get over one thing and move on to another. They're always griping or complaining about something. The problem is, people who are often angry become bitter people. Bitter people rarely keep it to themselves—they want to spread it around.

If you or your spouse fit this description, beware. It will infect your marriage and can also spread to your children and to others in your life. The Bible warns about a root of bitterness that can spring up and defile many (see Hebrews 12:15). Don't let bitterness overtake your marriage.

Have you been wronged? Has someone hurt you? Has someone said something unkind about you? Perhaps it was your spouse. You need to forgive him or her. "But they don't deserve it," you say. Regardless of what someone has said or done to us, the Bible tells us, "And be kind to one another, tenderhearted, forgiving one another, even as God in Christ forgave you" (Ephesians 4:32).

You should extend forgiveness because God has extended forgiveness to you. When you forgive someone, you set a prisoner free: *yourself*. When you harbor bitterness, you are hurting yourself. You are hurting other people. You aren't helping anything. Let it go. Forgive. Put it behind you. Don't carry it any further.

Quiet Please

In addition to being slow to get angry, we should be slow to speak, which is really the thrust of what James is saying in these verses. A major part of self-control is mouth control.

It's difficult to put your foot in your mouth when it's closed. That's something to think about. If we just would be quick to listen and slow to speak, we would avoid so much unnecessary misery. The Bible teaches that one day we will be held accountable for what we have said.

Jesus said, "But I say to you that for every idle word men may speak, they will give account of it in the day of judgment. For by your words you will be justified, and by your words you will be condemned" (Matthew 12:36–37).

Most of us speak a great many words in the course of our lives. It has been estimated that people speak enough words in one week to fill a 500-page book. But a true test of your faith is not the ability to speak your mind, but to hold your tongue. James is saying that if you want to be a spiritually mature person, you'll do it by learning to control your words. That is why the psalmist said, "I will watch what I do and not sin in what I say. I will curb my tongue when the ungodly are around me" (Psalm 39:1, NLT). We need to think about what we say, because there are many ways we can misuse our words.

Here is something to THINK about when you are talking to your husband, wife, or anyone, for that matter. When you are in doubt about something you're about to say, apply this test:

T   Is it *true?*

H   Is it *helpful?*

I   Is it *inspiring?*

N   Is it *necessary?*

K   Is it *kind?*

You might be saying, "Give me a break! If I applied these standards, I'd have to eliminate 90 percent of what I say!"

Then so be it.

Understand, even godly men and women struggle with keeping this area under control. Some of the greatest people that God ever used struggled with it. So don't feel like you're the only one.

Take Job, for instance. God Himself called Job "blameless and upright" (see Job 1:8). Yet even Job had trouble controlling his own tongue. He said, "I am nothing—how could I ever find the answers? I will put my hand over my mouth in silence. I have said too much already" (Job 40:4, NLT).

Isaiah was one of God's choice servants, but when he came into God's presence, the first things he became aware of was his words—and how he used his tongue. He said, "Woe is me, for I am undone! Because I am a man of unclean lips, and I dwell in the midst of a people of unclean lips; for my eyes have seen the King, the Lord of hosts" (Isaiah 6:5). When Isaiah was in the presence of God, he immediately became aware of the fact that he had misused his words and his tongue.

Use Them Wisely

We've learned how not to use our words and our tongue. So how should we use them?

We should use them to glorify God.

This is the highest and greatest use of our tongue because we were created to glorify God and give Him pleasure. The Apostle James notes: "With the tongue we praise our Lord and Father, and with it we curse men, who have been made in God's likeness. Out of the same mouth come praise and cursing. My brothers, this should not be" (James 3:9-10, NIV).

It's important to remember that we were put on this earth to bring honor and praise to the One who created us—and one of the ways we can accomplish that is through what we say.

Scripture overflows with examples of verbal praise to God. David wrote, "Because Your lovingkindness is better than life, my lips shall praise You. Thus I will bless You while I live; I will lift up my hands in Your name" (Psalm 63:3–4). Ephesians 5:18–19 (NLT) tells us, "Let the Holy Spirit fill and control you. Then you will sing psalms and hymns and spiritual songs among yourselves, making music to the Lord in your hearts."

Hebrews 13:15 (NLT) says, "With Jesus' help, let us continually offer our sacrifice of praise to God by proclaiming the glory of his name." God wants you to verbally glorify His name.

We should use our words to build up one another—first and foremost, our husband or wife.

The Bible says, "And let us not neglect our meeting together, as some people do, but encourage and warn each other, especially now that the day of his coming back again is drawing near" (Hebrews 10:25, NLT). We need to encourage one another. We need to correct one another.

I believe the Lord wants us to reevaluate how we use our words with our spouse. Let's use them for the right reasons: to glorify God and to build up one another. Let's not use them for tearing down each other. Let's ask God to give us the strength in our marriages to use our words for His glory.

Questions for Discussion

1. Why is the tongue "the world's most dangerous weapon"?

2. Greg writes: *"Most of us can remember hurtful words and taunts from the earliest days of childhood. Years and decades may roll by, but simply recalling those harsh or degrading words has the power to bring pain to the soul."*

Is that true for you? Can you recall negative or demeaning words spoken to you as a child or young person that you remember to this day? Now, to view the other side of this issue, can you remember positive, encouraging words someone spoke to you that you have treasured through your life?

3. James writes: *"My dear brothers and sisters, be quick to listen, slow to speak, and slow to get angry"* (James 1:19, NLT).

What does it mean to be "quick to listen"? What steps can we take to improve in that area?

4. What about the biblical counsel to be "slow to speak"? What habits or practices you would need to change to follow this advice? What additional insights can we gather from Proverbs 18:13 and 29:20?

5. James tells us we should be "slow to get angry." As Proverbs 29:11 says, "A fool gives full vent to anger, but a wise person quietly holds it back" (NLT). Galatians 5:19 speaks of "outbursts of wrath." What is the source of these outbursts? Reading 5:22-25, what is the biblical solution?

6. Unresolved anger that is allowed to fester may soon to turn to bitterness of heart. What does Hebrews 12:15 say in warning about bitterness? How can we remove these harmful feelings from our marriage relationship?

7. The Bible commands us to "be kind to one another, tenderhearted, forgiving one another, even as God in Christ forgave you" (Ephesians 4:32). What are some truths or characteristics about the way God forgave us in Christ? How then do we forgive others in the same way?

8. Greg writes: *"It's difficult to put your foot in your mouth when it's closed."*

Jesus was more specific, when He said, *"But I say to you that for every idle word men may speak, they will give account of it in the day of judgment. For by your words you will be justified, and by your words you will be condemned"* (Matthew 12:36–37).

If we really stopped to consider the above Scripture, how might it change the course of our comments and conversation in the course of a day?

9. Read Isaiah 6:5. What distressed Isaiah the most when he suddenly found himself in the presence of God? What was the first thing he felt he had to deal with? Would the content of our conversations change if we invested time in the morning to seeking God's nearness and presence?

10. Hebrews 15:13 (NLT) says, *"With Jesus' help, let us continually offer our sacrifice of praise to God by proclaiming the glory of his name."*

What do you think about the writer's use of the word "continually"? How do we continually offer praise to God through our day? How might we accomplish that?

CHAPTER 11

Duty: The Forgotten Word

Friends, don't slack off in doing your duty.
–2 Thessalonians 3:13, THE MESSAGE

It's a word that has fallen on hard times.

If you had spoken it to men and women in earlier generations—whether to a king in his castle, a soldier in the field, or the scullery maid in the kitchen—they would have known exactly what you meant, and many would have nodded their heads in recognition.

If you use the word today, most people won't even know what you're talking about—or if they do, they won't care.

Once upon a time, it was a word that was an animating, galvanizing, strengthening force to our forefathers and foremothers.

Jesus Himself used the word, in a few verses we'll be looking at in a moment. But it's not a passage you hear quoted very often anymore.

The word is *duty*, and apart from emergency responders or members of the military, it's not a term that most of us think about in the twenty-first century.

But maybe we should.

And maybe we should think about that word particularly in terms of marriage, family and the home.

We live in such self-absorbed times that the idea of doing something simply because it's the right thing to do has fallen out of favor. Nowadays the mentality is, *What's right for ME? What's in it for ME? What about MY needs?*

This is one of the reasons that marriages and families are so rapidly failing in our day. We'll say, "My mate no longer satisfies my needs. I'm no longer happy in this marriage." Then perhaps, we even have the temerity to drag God into it, saying, "God wants me to be happy. God wouldn't want me to stay in a marriage where I'm no longer fulfilled and content."

But wait a second. What about the commitment that you made? What about doing your duty as a Christian husband or wife? What about those vows that you stated one to another when you said you took that person for better or for worse, for richer or poorer, in sickness and in health, to love and to cherish until death you parted?

What about duty?

The dictionary defines duty as "something that one is expected or required to do by moral or legal obligation."

Does that have a harsh sound in your ears? Do you find words like "expected" or "required" just a little hard to swallow? It was different a hundred—maybe even fifty—years ago.

Civil War General Robert E. Lee wrote: "Duty is the most sublime word in our language. Do your duty in all things. You cannot do more. You should never wish to do less."

The 19th-century preacher Henry Ward Beecher put it poetically: "He who is false to present duty breaks a thread in the loom, and will find the flaw when he may have forgotten its cause."

The Book of Common prayer spoke of daily life in these terms: "To do my duty in that state of life unto which it shall please God to call me."

Johann Goethe said: "But what is your duty? What the day demands."

Finally, some unknown individual said these words that have somehow lasted through the years: "If I do my full duty, the rest will take care of itself."[32]

That is something we have forgotten about in this day and age. We need to be reminded that there are duties we have as believers.

There are duties that go along with being a husband or a wife, a father or a mother.

It seems people don't want to do their duty anymore. It's as though they feel that the world owes them something. Mark Twain said, "Don't go around saying the world owes you a living. The world owes you nothing. It was here first."[33]

Just saying the word "duty" reminds me of jury duty. I have been called—and served—many times. A number of years ago, John, one of our associate pastors at Harvest Fellowship, received a summons to serve on jury duty.

But he didn't want to go. He was busy, it wasn't convenient, and he didn't want to hassle with it. So he told me, "I'm just going to write them a letter and tell them I can't do it."

"John," I said, "you can't do that. You have to have a legitimate reason for avoiding jury duty. You can't just not show up. You have to contact the court and ask them for permission to be relieved."

But John wouldn't believe it. Why should he be bothered? He didn't want to do it. He wrote his letter and said he was just too busy.

That's when I decided to play a little trick on John. We made arrangements with one of the Christian cops in our church to have John "arrested" for avoiding jury duty. It was all a joke, of course, but he didn't know that.

John came walking out of church one Sunday morning with a big smile on his face, and there waiting for him was a uniformed member of the LAPD. If you're not from Southern California, you may not know this, but you never want to mess around with the LAPD. You might say they take life very seriously. With a face that was expressionless as a stone, this cop walked up to John and said, "Is your name…?" and gave John's full name.

"Yes, it is," John said.

The policeman said, "I hereby place you under arrest for avoidance of your lawful jury duty."

John looked around, trying to find the joke. "This is a joke, right?"

But the L.A. cop actually put him against the car, put John's hands behind his back and cuffed him! I was watching all of this, of course, and beginning to wonder if it had all gone a little too far. I was actually starting to feel sorry for my friend.

Then the policeman put him into the back of the squad car, and closed the door. And John wasn't smiling anymore.

I thought to myself, *I think it's time to put an end to this*. So I walked up to the policeman and said, "Excuse me, officer. But I think it's okay. We can stop this now."

The cop looked me square in the eyes and said, "You, back off."

I backed off.

For whatever reason, the LAPD officer kept John in the back of his squad car for ten more minutes before finally releasing him with a little smile.

I think John will show up for jury duty next time!

In Luke 17 we have the call of our Lord to do our duty as Christians. The problem is, many of us are reluctant to embrace that word—even when it's Jesus who speaks it. And even when it applies to our relationship with the people we love most.

> *Suppose one of you had a servant plowing or looking after the sheep. Would he say to the servant when he comes in from the field, 'Come along now and sit down to eat'? Would he not rather say, 'Prepare my supper, get yourself ready and wait on me while I eat and drink; after that you may eat and drink'? Would he thank the servant because he did what he was told to do? So you also, when you have done everything you were told to do, should say, 'We are unworthy servants; we have only done our duty'.* (Luke 17:7-10, NIV)

We must remember that as Christians we are the purchased property of Jesus Christ. On more than one occasion the Bible likens us to slaves. It's as if we were in an open slave market, and Jesus comes and bids for our freedom. He pays the price. Then He takes us into His own service. We were formerly slaves to sin under the power of Satan, the prince of the power of the air. But then Jesus purchased our freedom with His own blood.

Now, we are to serve Him.

From the day that we put our faith in Jesus Christ, we became

His purchased property. Amplifying on this theme, 1 Corinthians 6:20 says: "You were bought with a price, therefore glorify God in your body and in your spirit, which are God's."

For all practical purposes, when you became a Christian, God attached His ID tag to you. When I travel, I usually take a suitcase or two. I have a tendency to over-pack and take too many things with me. When I go to the baggage carousel, my bag will inevitably be the last one to come down the chute. Even so, I always check the luggage tag. I don't want to be loading someone else's things into my car and driving home with them. But just one glance at that ID tag confirms that this piece of luggage belongs to me.

When you became a follower of Jesus Christ, He attached His ID tag to you. We can see this truth highlighted in Ephesians 1:13-14.

In Him you also trusted, after you heard the word of truth, the gospel of your salvation; in whom also, having believed, you were sealed with the Holy Spirit of promise, who is the guarantee of our inheritance until the redemption of the purchased possession, to the praise of His glory.

The passage says I have been "sealed with the Holy Spirit of promise." What does that mean? Back in biblical times, when goods were shipped from one place to another, they would be stamped with a wax seal imprinted with a signet ring bearing a unique mark of ownership. If you saw a crate that had a wax seal with the king's imprint, you certainly wouldn't want to mess with that. In fact, you'd want to avoid all appearance of interfering with that piece of cargo, because a violation might well mean your life.

In the same way, God has placed His very own imprint on our life—His ID tag, if you will. I don't think we begin to understand what weight that carries in the universe. For instance, when the devil wants to come and make havoc of your life, he is stopped cold because he sees that seal of ownership.

Let's say you're a thief in an airport, you want to steal something, and you spot a very expensive briefcase on the conveyer belt. You look around, and nobody seems to be claiming the case. What a prize it would be! It has gold-plated hinges, and the handle is studded with diamonds. You say to yourself, *Wow, that case alone is valuable. Imagine what's in it!*

As you walk over to it, intending to quickly steal it and walk away, you notice an ID tag attached to it. It has the word "Tyson" on it.

You think, *Tyson? As in Tyson chicken?*

Then you see a very large, muscular man, half of his face tattooed, walking toward you, and you realize it's *Mike* Tyson, the professional fighter, who owns that briefcase. As a result, you decide to walk away and leave it alone. Why? Because you enjoy life. And you fear the owner.

In the same way, the devil—the one who has come "to steal, and to kill, and to destroy" (John 10:10)—approaches you. In his hatred and malice, he says, "I will wreak havoc in this life. I will ruin this person. I'll—wait, is that an ID tag? What does it say? 'Property of the Lord Jesus Christ? Purchased with His blood'? Uh-oh." And he backs off.

Satan does not have free reign to attack and destroy a son or daughter of God, because we have been sealed with the Holy Spirit of promise. God has put His ID tag on you, which is an incredible privilege.

But with that privilege comes responsibility.

Responsibilities Come With the Territory

I raised two wonderful sons, including one who is now with the Lord. As my boys grew up, they had all the privileges that went with being the sons of Greg and Cathe Laurie. They had a roof over their heads, food, clothing, skateboards, and whatever they needed. They had open and free access to me whenever they wanted it. If they were in trouble, I would be there for them. They knew I was always in their corner. Those were the privileges that came with relationship, as sons to their dad.

With those privileges there were also some responsibilities. In fact, as the boys were growing up, I would often give them tasks and instruct them what to do. I wouldn't say, "Would you please—just for me—take out the trash?" No, as their dad, I simply told them to do this or that. And most of the time they did!

Why did I say it that way? Simply put, to get things done. We had a household to run, and each of us had a part to play. As a parent, I was responsible to see that as my boys grew up they knew how to help, contribute and carry their own weight. Besides that, we had a relationship. I could speak to them that way, because of the relationship of intimacy we already had as father and sons. They had no problem with getting simple marching orders from their dad; they expected it.

But I can't do that with a total stranger. I can't stop someone walking by my house and say, "Hey, you. Come in here and take out the trash." I'd like to, but I really can't do that, because I have no relationship with that person. But I had the right to tell my own sons what to do, and to expect them to do it.

In the same way here in our text, God addresses us as His sons and daughters. He is essentially saying, "As My own children, you have all of the privileges and perks that come with relationship. You have My presence. You have My blessing. You have open access to Me 24/7. But you also have responsibilities. As my children, there are certain things that I expect of you. I want you to do what I tell you to do."

This is what Jesus is saying in Luke 17:9.

"Would he thank the servant because he did what he was told to do?"

No, He isn't obliged to do that. We belong to Him. We're His servants.

Here's another way to look at it: The very fact that Jesus would call upon us and tell us to do something should thrill our hearts. Why? Because it's a mark of ownership. He feels, and rightly so, that as your Father who has purchased your life with precious blood, He can call upon you to do something, and He expects your obedience. In essence, you have already agreed to this by accepting His salvation and forgiveness. You committed yourself to this when you said "yes" to Jesus Christ.

Interestingly, as you read many of Paul's New Testament letters, you'll see that he often opens with the phrase, "Paul, a servant of Jesus Christ." The word he uses for "servant" could better be translated as "bondslave." We may not understand the significance of that term, but they certainly did in the first century. A bondslave was a servant who had been freed, and then chose to serve willingly.

In other words, you're like that slave bought in the auction. You serve your master for seven years, then he lets you go. In response, you say, "Master, I love you so much that I don't want to leave you. I want to become your voluntary slave now. I want to be a bondslave." That would be indicated by a mark they would make in the lobe of your ear. From that time forward, anyone who saw you would know that you were a servant by choice—a voluntary slave to a master you loved more than your own life.

Paul would say, "I am a bondslave." The same is absolutely true of us, and there can be no quibbling or negotiating in this area. It is our duty to do what God tells us to do. Let me add that a true follower of Jesus should want to do His will. As soon as he knows what it is, he should gladly jump in and do it. If you know the will of God, then as a Christian, you should be happy that you know it, and you should just get out and do it.

People will often write me very nice letters and e-mails and say complimentary things to me after a church service. (I also get mean or even threatening letters and e-mails. But the nice ones outnumber those by far.) People will say things like,

"Greg, I really appreciate what you do."

"Greg, I thank God that you preach the Gospel and teach the Word."

"Thank you for your work, Greg. Thank you for your sacrifice."

Now those are nice words, and I appreciate being appreciated as much as anyone does. But the truth is, I'm only doing my duty—just as you are doing your duty. Neither of us deserve any special thanks, because we're doing what God has called us to do.

I'll let you in on a little secret, however. It is my great privilege and joy to do what I do. I enjoy it thoroughly. I take great delight in doing the duty that God has called me to do. And I hope you have the same attitude toward what He has called you to do.

Having established the fact that we are to do our duty, what *is* our duty specifically?

In the context of the book you have just completed, we have a duty to our marriage, and a duty to our family.

Do the Right Thing

You say, "I still don't like that word 'duty,' Greg. I prefer to say that I have the privilege or the opportunity or the pleasure of caring for my spouse, and staying faithful to my vows."

Yes, I would say the same thing.

But sometimes, when life gets pulled this way and that… when we're feeling overwhelmed, undervalued, burned-out, or brokenhearted…when we can no longer "feel" much of anything and care even less…we still have a duty to our spouse and our children. We need to do the right thing by our family simply because it is the right thing.

Ultimately, we need to do it because we belong—heart, body and soul—to Jesus Christ, and as our Lord, it's what He expects of us.

What sort of duties? I'm talking about the biblical imperatives we've just reviewed in these pages.

- *Therefore be imitators of God as dear children. And walk in love, as Christ also has loved us and given Himself for us…"*
- *"Wives, submit to your own husbands, as to the Lord."*
- *"Husbands, love your wives, just as Christ also loved the church and gave Himself for her…"*
- *"Children, obey your parents in the Lord, for this is right."*
- *"Husbands, in the same way be considerate as you live with your wives, and treat them with respect as the weaker partner and as*

heirs with you of the gracious gift of life."

- *"Husbands, love your wives and do not be harsh with them."*
- *"And you, fathers, do not provoke your children to wrath, but bring them up in the training and admonition of the Lord."*
- *"Submit to one another out of reverence for Christ."*
- *"Nevertheless let each one of you in particular so love his own wife as himself."*
- *"Let the wife see that she respects her husband."*
- *"The husband should fulfill his marital duty to his wife, and likewise the wife to her husband. The wife's body does not belong to her alone but also to her husband. In the same way, the husband's body does not belong to him alone but also to his wife."*
- *"If anyone does not provide for his relatives, and especially for his immediate family, he has denied the faith and is worse than an unbeliever."*[34]

What, then, are these commands? Are they incredible privileges...or duties? The answer is they're *both*. And they're still duties even when they don't feel like privileges!

We need to love and provide and protect and submit and cherish and respect our mates because Jesus expects us to.

You don't want to? You don't feel like it? You're not motivated? *So what?*

Do those things anyway, as unto Jesus. The One who shed His blood for you and laid down His life for you has every right to expect full-hearted obedience of His bondslaves.

But here's the little secret. The more you do, for your family, and as unto Him, the sweeter life becomes. Happiness slips in through the back door, and stays a long, long time.

Questions for Discussion

1. Before you read this chapter, what would your first impressions of the word "duty" have been?

2. Greg writes: *"We live in such self-absorbed times that the idea of doing something simply because it's the right thing to do has fallen out of favor. Nowadays the mentality is, 'What's right for ME? What's in it for ME? What about MY needs?'"*

Do you agree with this statement? What evidence of this attitude have you seen within the last few weeks?

3. *"God wants me to be happy. God wouldn't want me to stay in a marriage where I'm no longer fulfilled and content."*

If one of your friends or loved ones was in an immoral relationship and came to you with the above argument, how would you counter it? What Scriptures might you use?

4. Greg writes: *"There are duties that go along with being a husband or a wife, a father or a mother."*

Does the word "duty" make your think of drudgery…or privilege and opportunity? How much have are we influenced by our contemporary culture as we seek to process this concept of "duty"?

5. Read Luke 17:7-10. What do you think the Lord wants us to learn from these verses? What wrong or harmful heart-attitude might the Lord be addressing with these words?

6. Greg writes: *"From the day that we put our faith in Jesus Christ, we became His purchased property."*

What does the Lord remind us of in 1 Corinthians 6:20?

7. Read Ephesians 1:13-14. What are the implications of wearing the Lord Jesus' ID tag through all of life? List as many as you can.

8. Greg writes: *"Satan does not have free reign to attack and destroy a son or daughter of God, because we have been sealed with the Holy Spirit of promise. God has put His ID tag on you, which is an incredible privilege."*

But what are the responsibilities that go along with this privilege?

9. Greg writes that because the Father purchased our lives at the cost of His Son's precious blood, He has a full right to expect our obedience. *"In essence,"* he says, *"you have already agreed to this by accepting His salvation and forgiveness."*

How would you apply this truth to your marriage, and the specific directions for wives and husbands that we have seen in this book?

10. Ultimately, we need to carefully follow the Bible's instructions to us as husbands and wives because we belong—heart, body and soul—to Jesus Christ, and as our Lord, it's what He expects of us. How can we make sure that our obedience to Christ is a choice of the heart, as well as an expectation and a duty?

Conclusion

But may all who search for you be filled with joy and gladness. –Psalm 70:4, NLT

Little girls grow up wanting to be princesses, and longing for a prince to come rescue them. Boys grow up with the romantic notion of meeting some beautiful girl who will adore them and meet the deepest needs of their life.

You can hear it in popular music, going back as far as life. We long for someone to complete us, to be with us, to understand us, to fulfill us, and to bring significance to our lives. In the movie *Shall We Dance*, one of the characters expressed it like this: "We need a witness to our lives. There's a billion people on the planet. … I mean, what does anyone's life really mean? But in a marriage, you're promising to care about everything. The good things, the bad things, the terrible things, the mundane things—all of it, all of the time, every day. You're saying, 'Your life will not go unnoticed, because I will notice it. Your life will not go un-witnessed, because I will be your witness.'"

God in His kindness to humanity gave men and women to each other to comfort us, help us and fulfill us, and we certainly praise Him for that. Apart from Jesus Christ Himself, Cathe is the most wonderful gift God has ever given to me.

But deep down at the very core of our souls, beyond any other human longing, what you and I really long for is God Himself.

A man can sometimes please and fulfill a woman, and a woman can sometimes please and fulfill a man. But a man can't do everything or be everything for a woman, and a woman can't do everything or be everything for a man.

In some pop-music song, a guy or a girl will sing "you are my world" or "you are my everything." It sounds romantic and sweet and all that, but God never intended one man or one woman to fill up all the empty places in our soul. No one person could do that. No one person should ever be expected to do that.

No one but God alone.

Someone has well said, "Never expect man to do for you what only God can do. And don't confuse the two!"

Our Father in heaven is the One we really long for.

Jesus is the wonderful Prince who has come to rescue us, and will come again to receive us to Himself.

The Holy Spirit is the One who will be with us through all of life—"closer than hands or feet, closer than breathing."[35] He will be that witness that our hearts long for. He will fill the empty days and the lonely moments with His own presence and nearness and wisdom and conversation and cheer.

We were created to know God. And whether we are married, single, divorced or widowed, He will be our Companion and Friend and Defender, and help us to become all we were created to be.

Life with Christ begins when you admit you are a sinner, and you cry out to Him, asking for His help and His forgiveness. Then Christ Himself will come and live inside of you, and give you the strength to be the man or the woman God has called you to be, whatever your marital status.

But if you are married, He will enable you to become the husband your wife dreams of, or He will empower you to become the wife your longs for. There is no sin He can't forgive, no obstacle He can't overcome, and no empty place He can't fill.

New life begins today, as you look to Him and say, "Lord, I need You."

Endnotes

1. Manser, Martin H. *The Facts on File Dictionary of Proverbs* (New York: Infobase, 2007), 159.

2. Song of Solomon 8:7

3. Waite, Linda L. and Maggie Gallagher. *The Case for Marriage* (New York: Broadway Books, 2000).

4. Quoted in: Graham, Jack and Deb. *Courageous Parenting* (Wheaton: Crossway, 2006), 19.

5. Jackson, Wayne. "The Devasting Effects of Divorce." Accessed at: http://www.christiancourier.com/articles/81-the-devastating-effects-of-divorce.

6. Horn, Wade F. *Father Facts: Third Edition*. The National Fatherhood Initiative. Accessed at http://www.fafny.org/FamilyHelpPDFfiles/17-Father-Facts.pdf.

7. Churchill, Winston S. *Never Give In!* (New York: Hyperion, 2003), 214.

8. Dobson, James. *Love for a Lifetime: Building a Marriage That Will Go the Distance* (Sisters: Multnomah Publishers, 2004), 42-43.

9. *Ibid*

10. 2 Timothy 2:19, NIV

11. John 3:22

12. Ephesians 1:6

13. 1 Peter 3:7, NASB

14. Barclay, William. *The Letters of James and Peter* (Louisville: Westminster John Knox Press, 2003), 251.

15. Hopcke, Robert H. and Paul A. Schwartz. *Little Flowers of Francis of Assisi* (Boston: New Seeds Books, 2006), 3.

16. Swindoll, Charles R. *Growing Strong in the Seasons of Life* (Grand Rapids: Zondervan, 1983), 60.

17. Love, Patricia and Steven Stosny. *How to Improve Your Marriage Without Talking About It* (New York: Broadway, 2007), 49.

18. Hyatt, Michael. "Top Selling Christian Books of 2010". Accessed at: http://michaelhyatt.com/the-100-bestselling-christian-books-of-2010.html (comments section).

19. 1 Peter 3:7, KJV

20. Henry, Matthew. *Matthew Henry's Commentary on the Whole Bible* (Peabody Hendrickson, 1996), Genesis 2:21.

21. Wiersbe, Warren. *The Wiersbe Bible Commentary: New Testament* (Colorado Springs: David C. Cook, 2007), 56.

22. Pope John Paul II. *A Pilgrim Pope: Messages for the World* (Kansas City: McMeel, 1999), 318.

23. Wallerstein, Judith S. and Sandra Blakeslee. *Second Chances* (New York: Houghton Mifflin, 1996).

24. Accessed at: http://www.enduringword.com/commentaries/4019.htm.

25. Weitzman, Lenore J. *The Divorce Revolution* (Glencoe: Free Press, 1985).

26. Kantrowitz, Barbara. "Breaking The Divorce Cycle". *Newsweek.* January 13, 1992.

27. O'Donnell, Jayne and Greg Farrell. "Business scandals prompt look into personal lives." *USA TODAY.* November 5, 2004. Accessed at http://www.usatoday.com/money/companies/management/2004-11-05-white-collar-sex_x.htm.

28. Ten Boom, Corrie. *Tramp for the Lord* (New York: Berkeley, 1974), 48.

29. Vaughan, Peggy. *The Monogamy Myth* (New York: Newmarket Press, 2003), 7.

30. "The Odds are Against You'. *Spy.* The New York Monthly. March, 1987, 47.

31. Johnson, Alan F. *1 Corinthians* (Downers Grove: InterVarsity, 2004), 17.

32. All "duty" quotes can be accessed at: http://www.worldofquotes.com/topic/Duty/1/index.html.

33. Accessed at: http://www.worldofquotes.com/author/Mark+Twain/12/index.html.

34. Ephesians 5:1-2; 5:22; 5:25; 6:1; 1 Peter 3:7 (NIV); Colossians 3:19 (NIV); Ephesians 6:4; Ephesians 5:21 (NIV); Ephesians 5:33; Ephesians 5:33; 1 Corinthians 7:3-5 (NIV); 1 Timothy 5:8 (NIV)

35. Jeremiah, David. *God In You* (Sisters: Multnomah Publishers, 1998), 102.

Greg Laurie Books with Study Guides

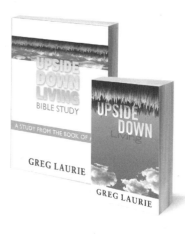

Other Books by Greg Laurie

KERYGMA
PUBLISHING

Visit: www.AllenDavidBooks.com